AN AMERICAN
DIVORCE

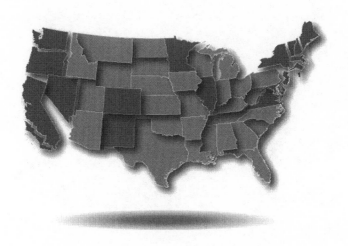

J. N. Welch

Author: J.N. Welch

Copyright © 2019 by William H. Honaker, The IP Guy.

3rd Edition republished February 2022.

CONTENTS

J. N. Welch

As an organizer, I start from where the world is, as it is, not as what I would like it to be. That we accept the world as it is does not weaken our desire to change it into what we believe it should be...
—*Saul Alinsky*

The **Second Edition** of *An American Divorce* was published in April 2021 to reflect the 2020 US presidential election results. During this revision process, the author edited each respective chapter.

The **Third Edition of *An American Divorce*** was published in February 2022 to reflect an election year in US politics. A new chapter was added to the book. (Chapter 13) No other edits were made to the book beyond page sequencing, table of contents and cover modification(s), and the segue into the new chapter.

J. N. Welch

Chapter I: Going Back to College

When two people decide to get a divorce, it isn't that they don't understand one another, but a sign that they have, at last, begun to.
—*Helen Rowland*

All of us can feel the division and dysfunction, but we don't know where to begin the conversation. When the US experienced *divorce* in the 1860s, most Americans understood what the breakup was ultimately about.

Today, things are not quite as simple.

We're not listening to Civil War rivals like Stephen Douglas and Abraham Lincoln lay out dueling platforms with moral and intellectual clarity. In today's *woke* environment, careers are lost and reputations are destroyed overnight, simply for saying the wrong thing to the wrong person.

And anyone who dares to challenge the conventional wisdom of the elites is deemed to be an unenlightened lightweight, or even a personal threat, to those select groups who meet today's politically correct criteria of being "disadvantaged."

In a world with big problems and complex challenges, we are often left with these types of questions at our prized American universities:

7

- Should disadvantaged college students be afforded "safe zones" to feel more comfortable in their well-being?
- Should human beings continue using words like "man" and "woman?" Or should gender identity be a fluid and individual choice?
- Do White people understand their consciousness is flawed because of privilege?

The United States of America has come full circle as a civilization. The country that was first to walk away from authoritarian rule is, today, powerless to confront the tyranny found in its own back yard.

I grew up in a lower/middle-income neighborhood. My politics were first influenced by my grandfather's love of Franklin Roosevelt and John F. Kennedy. On Sunday mornings, we would listen to FDR's fireside chats on those old LP albums. I still find emotion in the charisma and confidence both presidents displayed during some very difficult times in America.

After graduating from high school, I went off to college. Thirty-seven years later, though, I can still remember the first spoken words from an early morning philosophy class. After strolling into class late, the professor carefully scanned the room and declared, *"Boy, it's colder than a nun's cunt outside!"*

Later in that same class, he proclaimed:

All of you are being held in intellectual shackles. Your parents may be nice people, but they are simply pawns—tending to their lawns, obeying their bosses, and raising their flags on patriotic holidays. You, on the other hand, are going to have an opportunity your parents never had; you're going to find liberation from the hypocrisy and illusion of what America really stands for.

We all have that moment in life when we first contemplate our parents are not perfect. I still remember going home from college after that first day and looking down on my mom and dad.

I felt sorry for them and their simple ways.

Several years later, I quit college to take over a failing family business. I was no longer in the theoretical environment of a classroom and soon began to realize my parents weren't the simpletons the philosophy instructor had first led me to believe.

I was working on construction crews and quickly got a taste of life outside the classroom. Whether one lives near a city such as Oakland, Baltimore, or Cleveland, most of us have become immune to a local news cycle almost certain to begin with an overnight smash-and-grab, abduction, or homicide. Unfortunately, I saw the harsh reality of inner-city life on the first day of the job. While riding up an elevator in a public housing complex, I stood side-by-side as the elevator attendant and a building occupant got into a knife fight.

And the fun didn't end in the elevator.

In the suburbs where I grew up, random women would never proposition me into their apartments for sex. In that HUD facility, however, every day would feature the same morning routine. As I walked through the halls with other crewmembers, women would stand in front of their doorways, asking the younger guys to come inside for a "quickie." Many of these women had no qualms with their openness, while four or five children stood behind them in the doorway.

Before college, I had never seen a house on fire. In the low-rent districts, however, it wasn't uncommon to see one or two houses burning every week.

And to this day, if you're not careful picking the right gas station beyond the heavily policed areas, there is a reasonable chance you will become the next statistic from a violent carjacking.

After spending a decade going through the normal ebb and flow associated with growing a business, I decided to return to the university to finish what I couldn't complete in the 1980s. I began college when Ronald Reagan was president and graduated when Barack Obama was two years into his presidency.

In what could best be explained as a Rodney Dangerfield, *Back to School* experience, it was fascinating to begin a day downtown and then finish the evening in an academic setting with progressive *intellectuals*.

To the professors, of course, every urban problem was always displaced back to White privilege, income inequality, and racism. Forget the fact I rarely saw fathers in any of those housing complexes. And forget the reality that many urban areas in the US look like a Mad Max setting of dilapidated housing, abandoned automobiles, and random dump sites.

Those anecdotal observations simply had little relevance to any classroom discussion that didn't begin with *racism* and end with *privilege*.

I spent three decades sitting through a cult-like experience, and I understand the progressive mindset as if it were my own. There were even times when I would use their playbook to question my own belief systems:

- Was my conservative bent influenced by *privilege*?
- Did my experience as a construction worker make my masculinity *toxic*?
- Did my experiences in inner-city HUD projects make me a *racist*?

Our twenty-first-century intellectuals do have an impressive ledger of scholarly distinctions, and they know how to solve complex problems on paper. They have come to believe they are intellectually enlightened, and that Republican voters are a combination of racists, religious crazies, greedy millionaires and billionaires, or those who were dumb enough to vote for a president who lied every day.

For years, the conventional wisdom of most parents was to find any way to send the kids off to college. This method still works for those students who have the smarts and work ethic to become doctors, scientists, and engineers. But not many American kids have what it takes to get into the physical sciences, nor do they have what it takes to perform strenuous labor.

So, our high school graduates gravitate to the "cupcake" majors in college, and this is where the indoctrination begins.

Today, there are millions of millennials who view each personal failure through the lens of a perpetual struggle as a victim. Every hardship in life can be easily projected back onto capitalism, sexism, or racism. Every problem in the world can be intellectually displaced onto millionaires and billionaires, including the billions of dollars in student-debt loans tied to a piece of paper that has very little value in today's global economy.

The mindset of perpetual victimhood represents a beautiful psychology for those leaders who know how to use the leftist playbook. There are today millions of clueless *adults* who will go through life trying to merge personal inadequacies into a life-changing movement that seeks to find greater levels of *empathy, equality, and social justice.*

Bernie Sanders was an unaccomplished loner in Congress.

Yet, he could have easily won the US presidency in both 2016 and 2020. Sanders's success was most reflected in the sheer number of millennials who bought into the same

11

regurgitated nonsense I first heard at the university in the 1980s. True to Marxist form, Sanders was able to project every defect in life onto a billionaire bogeyman.

It is true this type of talk will come across as insensitive to those younger Americans who have bought into the logic that millionaires and billionaires are responsible for every problem in the world. Many college-educated millennials are oblivious to the cultural reality that lies beyond the ivy-covered university walls, the travel-abroad cities, and the watchful eyes of the local police departments.

When US students visit Paris, they go to the Louvre or the Eiffel Tower. They are not walking through the backstreets of Seine-Saint-Denis.

And when the kids go to Chicago for a weekend road trip, they're attending a Lollapalooza concert at Grant Park. They are not taking a stroll through the bad neighborhoods of Fuller Park.

In this era of safe zones and overprotective parents, younger Americans are simply not seeing the worst human nature has to offer. Unlike previous generations, these young adults are largely sheltered from war, communist dictators, and existential hardship. Many younger Americans also seem to have personal identities forged by what the *New York Times* columnist David Brooks refers to as the "culture of selfism," meaning, "a culture that puts tremendous emphasis on self, self-care, and self-display."

Rather than viewing morality as living up to external standards like honesty, courage, and patriotism, Brooks writes, "Traditional morality has been replaced by self-indignation, being heard, telling your story and then, of course, condemning the bad people that make you feel judged or sad."[i]

To Generations Y and Z, the imagery of racist cops, open borders, and White privilege makes perfect sense. These younger adults do not seem to understand why former mansions in cities like Detroit are presently selling for under ten thousand dollars.

Just as they don't seem to understand that the progressives who want to abolish entire police precincts today are the very same people who diminished the qualifications to become a police officer thirty years ago.

In recent times, the United States and other Western democracies have been significantly influenced by older Whites with little or no college education. While attending the university, it was always interesting being the only *older adult* in the classroom when the college professors would attempt the delicate task of reducing older Whites to unenlightened buffoons who watch Fox News every night. In that cat-and-mouse academic environment, I had to essentially defend "old and White" without *sounding* old and White.

Unlike the professors, however, older Americans have seen the before and after of the progressive blueprint in a real-world setting. They have watched their children and grandchildren become part of the lost generation, where self-esteem was promoted without real accomplishment, traditional morality was ridiculed, gender roles were flipped upside down, and the thought of being patriotic to your country was akin to being a country bumpkin.

The results of this social experiment are becoming very apparent to those real-world Americans who live up close and personal with modern-day progressivism in the workplace, in the schools, and in their neighborhoods. They see a world quite different from the utopia being extolled in the lecture seats at the Ivy Leagues.

Who is in the best position to witness the leftist experiment without bias? Is it the twenty-nine-year-old techie living in a *safe zone* downtown loft?

Or is it the working-class plumber who lives next door to a Section 8 public housing complex?

These latter Americans have the common sense to understand unlimited immigration and open borders will eventually break the glue that has bound the American identity together for centuries. And they also understand life will never be fair—or free.

Many of these working-class voters certainly don't trust Republicans, but they didn't have a better option in 2016. So they took a chance on the crazy guy for president because they were desperate. Are we living in a world in which the so-called elites were intellectually exposed by a segment of the US electorate that is the *least educated*? And if so, who are these millions of voters the Democrat elites are having such a hard time understanding?

Maybe it's the parents who worked their entire life for a college fund, only to see their daughter living back at home, angry, apathetic, and voting for politicians who hate the United States.

Or maybe it's those middle-class Americans who work and live where the social engineering plays out in real time. This may be the construction worker who works side-by-side with an unqualified worker who was placed on the jobsite simply to meet a racial quota.

Or it may be the factory worker who is the only one in the neighborhood who seems to go to work in the morning. Everyone else is on disability, collecting welfare, or living off their parents.

Trump's die-hard supporters are most likely to be Whites whose fathers and grandfathers fought in wars to protect liberty from tyranny, Latinos and Asians who escaped corrupt tyrants, and Blacks who understand the new master has some of the same qualities as the old master.

These Americans know there is more to criminal behavior than systematic racism and racist cops. They understand giving able-bodied people easy money will keep them in front of their

Xbox instead of finding a real job. This silent majority will listen to any politician who dares to speak up against the intellectual nonsense that has permeated nearly every corner of Western civilization. But these patriots also understand time is not on the side of putting God, country, and family ahead of wokeness, universal equality, and open borders.

There is an intellectual crisis occurring in Western civilization, and it may have been those with the least amount of education who exposed the folly. Any true intellectual should be worried when there is uniformity amongst one's peers. Today's monopoly of thought is not only arrogant; it represents the height of ignorance for any one person or group to think they have cornered the market on intelligence and knowledge. Just who can meet the scrutiny of having a real opinion without being labeled as racist, homophobic, or xenophobic?

Only they can.

The intellectuals of today have accomplished what the capitalist barons did during the Industrial Revolution. They have created their own monopoly in a day and age when society needs them to be free from dogma and unlimited in their ability to openly debate the great issues of our time.

The Democrats and Republicans *do* share something in common. Both have been inept at trying to implement their highest level of idealism. Conservatives haven't had a cohesive playbook since the 1980s. The establishment Republicans are the British redcoats of yesterday, standing in rigid formation and devoid of the know-how to fight back against a clever adversary. Their only hope now is that the strong personality of someone like Donald Trump can reverse the intellectual nonsense that has nearly split the US in two. The traditionalist should understand, however, that no individual will unite two worldviews that broke apart years ago. No single human being will be able to drain a swamp that has been polluted for decades with trillions of dollars and a revolving door between Wall Street and Washington, D.C.

Today's older Democrats are also starting to see how identity politics promote mass victimization, anger, and envy. Once the psychology of victimization is in place, there will be no bottom. The perpetual victim will seek endless ways to rationalize their personal shortcomings, and their corresponding anger can even turn full circle.

The original friend can become the new foe. It won't be long before the revenge of the victim classes moves beyond Christopher Columbus and over to FDR and JFK. The radicalized leftist(s) will always want more than what was originally offered, and they will become hostile when their place in society is not in alignment with their expectations of grandeur.

What is true in raising kids is also true in how a society is managed. When a child's past is rooted in guilt and their future is steered toward envy and entitlement, they will become angry toward others and doubtful of themselves. They will follow false prophets who purport to have easy answers to complex life problems. This is what we have done to a generation of millennials whose lives have been forged by being "liked" on Facebook, harboring guilt about their heritage, and not having any reliable moral code aside from expressing feelings and being in harmony with the planet.

We have allowed millions of individual psyches to become zombie-like, polluted by the politics of envy and robbed of the American spirit of taking big risks to accomplish great things.

By the end of my college journey, I knew the professors had found their winning hand. The Marxist academics have cleverly figured out how to embarrass and marginalize any voice that dares to speak out against the present-day assault on two-parent families, Judeo-Christian values, and limited government.

It is true the college-educated radicals have been around since the 1960s. Today, however, their reach is found everywhere in society. The education establishment has become monopolized, religion is in decline, and the strong family structure from previous generations has become unglued. Ignoring these developments and hoping America will find itself again is not going to be remedied using conventional tactics.

Throwing more money into urban areas to keep Blacks appeased is not going to work much longer. The original sin of slavery will no longer be reconciled with money and appeasement. Blacks now have enough money and representation to fight back against the dead White guys who still remain on the fifty and hundred-dollar bills.

I understand how talking this way has become very dangerous today; these kinds of conversations can trigger death threats, civil unrest, and maybe even a *societal divorce.*

Predicting revolutions is like predicting earthquakes. They are inevitable, but there is no crystal ball that can predict timing and outcome. But just as the Covid-19 pandemic demonstrated how quickly life can change without warning, mass paradigm changes in the human order can be equally sudden and often cruel.

The goal today is to get ahead of our marital dysfunction before things grow even worse. The US *could* pursue a divorce arrangement that is initially amicable to both sides. For every Texan who wants to secede from the Union, there is a Californian who feels the same way. There is also a chance both parties will simply continue to live in the passive-aggressive public arrangement we exist in now. This type of societal compact is common in other countries, including our docile neighbor to the north. Contrary to public belief, Canada is not a large geographic swath of endless cooperation and harmony. Canada's population of thirty-five million people actually consists of three distinct worldviews, and they, too, have had their own aspirations of breaking up.[ii]

Unlike Canada, the US plays a much larger role in the global community. If we continue to be an intellectually disconnected superpower that sends contradictory messages every time a new president is sworn in, the entire world order is at risk.

Worse yet, the global community may simply conclude the US is no longer a reliable partner. Should this second course of action play out, it will likely mean the democratic traditions advanced by the US will see a dramatic decline. The global community will eventually favor a consistent China over a politically impotent and unpredictable America.

Not long ago, it seemed like we had it all, but over time, our marriage began to change. At first, we ignored the boorish behavior. We assumed our partner was going through a temporary hurdle or maybe a midlife crisis. Instead of throwing in the towel, we decided to stick it out. We turned a blind eye to the arrogance and abuse, hoping everything would return to normal. But in tolerating the anger, we compromised who we once were.

We allowed ourselves to be dominated to the point of becoming irrelevant.

We allowed ourselves to be placed inside a dark box.

If it hasn't already become apparent, one side of the marriage has grown inflexible, angry, and violent. If left unchecked, the anger will consume anyone who stands in its way.

Yes, we also have our crazies.

But the leftist crazies now control how mainstream Americans think, feel, and behave. If we don't stop them, they could soon be within reach of bringing the entire house down.

An American Divorce isn't about a bunch of crazy rednecks shooting AK-47s in the backwoods. Our plan is to unite like-minded White, Black, and Brown Americans with the most powerful set of ideas the world has ever known. Ultimately, this book is about regaining the confidence to return to who we once were.

Our plan doesn't have to involve winning on every issue. In this sense, there is a chance a fresh and unfiltered conversation could salvage the marriage.

Just as there is also the chance a new conversation could lead to both sides agreeing to disagree and simply parting ways.

However, there is *also* the possibility that by talking on our terms, and not just theirs, they may become more violent than they already are today. Should this latter set of circumstances play out, we will consider putting them into the same dark place we are living in today.

Chapter 2: Why the Crazy Divorce Talk?

But I suppose the most revolutionary act one can engage in is... to tell the truth.

—*Howard Zinn*

The 1960s were a watershed moment in our marriage. In 1963, John F. Kennedy was assassinated, and to this day, we're not entirely certain how it happened.

Shortly after JFK's tragic death, America became involved in a war that should have never occurred. Vietnam took the lives of nearly sixty thousand American soldiers and two million Vietnamese.[iii] In justifying the war, generals, congressmen, and presidents lied.

In 1968, both Robert Kennedy and Martin Luther King Jr. were assassinated, and in 1972, a Republican president would resign over a Watergate scandal.

After two hundred years of unbridled confidence and optimism, cracks began to emerge in the American psyche. The glaring imperfections of the 1960s political establishment opened the door to the agitators and the Marxists. The counterculture knew in their heart of hearts there had to be a better way than endless war, racial inequality, LBJ, and Nixon.

Leftist agitators like Howard Zinn and Saul Alinsky found their opening in academia, and their influence has permeated throughout every segment of society ever since.

Before we open the "divorce" conversation, let's begin with some basic clarification. Political labels are fluid and change throughout the context of time. At this moment, I'm not even sure what it means to be a "Republican" or a "conservative."

Doesn't a fiscal *conservative* believe in balanced budgets?

Isn't a social *conservative* supposed to believe in only two genders and one type of marriage?

And wasn't the Republican Party once intended to represent both fiscal and social conservatives? If so, when did things begin to go sideways? What does it even mean to be a conservative or a Republican today?

And if we look closer at the Democrat side, what is the difference between a liberal, a progressive, or a Democratic Socialist?

Is a Democratic Socialist a communist revolutionary who believes in free elections?

Or is he/she a liberal who wants more socialism than capitalism?

Is the present-day Democrat Party intended to represent the interests of workers over bosses, or have the "progressives" shifted to a globalist platform that seeks to put the US Congress on equal status with the United Nations?

Yes, both political parties are going through their own respective identity crises. Moving forward, I will use words like "traditionalist" or "our side" or "we" to distinguish those Americans who believe capitalism, democratic values, limited government, and strong families are the gold standard in finding the highest order in human affairs.

A "traditionalist" is thus our protagonist, who, under the right set of mass-movement circumstances, would be willing to risk a *divorce* to help defeat the leftist "intelligentsia."

What do we mean by a "divorce" or a "mass movement"? Assuming the Democrats and Republicans are stuck in a dysfunctional marriage, what are the options when two groups of people can't seem to agree on anything?

They can essentially:

- Find common ground and remain in the marriage.
- Divorce their partner on good terms.
- Divorce their partner on bad terms.

Metaphorically speaking, our "divorce" goal *isn't* about helping Donald Trump and the Republicans. The "mass-movement" objective of the *traditionalist*, rather, is to assemble a widespread movement, which has the power to defeat an "ideological cancer" that has divided the US into a state of cultural and democratic paralysis.

The *cancer* in our marriage originated from those academics who have pitted millions of us against each other. If today's leftist elites and their enablers can be exposed and discredited, there exists the possibility the rest of us can begin to heal, unify, and find democratic normalcy. Moving forward, we will contemplate how this "good divorce" path could occur using mass-movement tactics in conjunction with a *new Republican Party*.

The *second divorce* option is associated with a geographical breakup of the United States. Assuming there are no *good divorce* options, what is the alternative? Is it possible the US could use a "Brexit-like" strategy where *red-* and *blue-*Americans simply agree to disagree, and then figure out a peaceful way to break the US into two separate countries?

The final divorce path(s) assume red- and blue-Americans remain stuck with no easy exit strategy for either side. From the perspective of the "traditionalist," this would imply a scenario where the leftists control the cultural norms, but *we* decide to *radically* challenge the power structure from inside the marriage.

Applying this concept to revolutionary theory, today's conservatives would learn how to become tomorrow's radicals.

In what would essentially become a zero-sum battle for control of the American identity, *we* would *agitate* the United States into a state of civil unrest and then hope to capitalize on the resulting chaos. Under this type of *mass-movement* scenario, the US military could play a significant role in the final divorce outcome.

Is it possible to expose our angry partner without conflict? Or is an American divorce destined to be *ugly* in outcome? These two questions should be thoroughly considered as we move through the questions of *why, who, and how.*

In trying to comprehend *why* the US is in such trouble, we need to begin by understanding what the *divorce fault lines* are really about. The long-standing dysfunction in Washington, D.C. goes much deeper than the talking points playing out on the twenty-four-hour news channels. Our underlying tensions are not rooted in race, taxation, abortion, foreign policy, or any other hot-button political issue(s).

Ultimately, our problems go back to age-old question(s) that have plagued philosophers for thousands of years.

Today's marital turbulence goes back to the fundamental philosophical question of *who* we are as people. Can human nature be perfected to guarantee future harmony to every person on the planet? Or do we live in a largely unknown reality where finding balance between benevolent and malevolent human impulses is the best way to advance the human condition?

Can life be free, fair, and *equal* in outcome? Or is the notion of universal equality an intellectual absurdity?

Is widespread cooperation possible, or is *globalism* a misguided philosophical leap that could ultimately lead to the marginalization and potential destruction of the United States of America?

Are our *educated* kids and their college professors correct— are traditional-minded parents simply unenlightened stooges who "cling to their guns and their religion" because they don't know any better?[iv] Or are guns and a strong belief in a higher power prerequisites in protecting individual liberty?

Until we realize where our marriage went wrong, it is silly to think there is going to be a game-changing breakthrough in Washington, D.C. now that Donald Trump has left the White House. Our marital troubles run deep, and they go far beyond Trump.

I'm not trying to win over the real *antagonist* with this book. I spent decades in their domain *as a minority*, and I understand what motivates them. Arrogance packaged as compassion, empathy, and "helping the greater good" rarely goes down without a real fight. The *devil* in our divorce story is not going to go away with mere words or self-help advice.[v]

Nor is there going to be some future moment in time when millions of progressive elites conclude, "We were wrong; thank you for enlightening us." This isn't how human nature works. Yes, human beings can cooperate and love in the most trying of circumstances, but at the opposite end of our existence lies another reality rooted in power, self-centeredness, and dominance. By failing to acknowledge the full spectrum of who we are as living beings, the "educated left" have essentially placed our country in great peril.

Today, college students ask me, "Why is socialism bad? What is so wrong with the way the Norwegian countries are doing things?" Or they ask, "Why is communism flawed?" Before we answer these types of questions, let's listen to the sermon in greater detail:

Professor to class:

Religion, nation-states, and capitalism have reduced the human existence to a zero-sum battle for power and dominance. Millions of innocent human beings have died in the name of religious purity, ethnic cleansing, and the pillaging of resources. Once human beings are conditioned to cooperate on a global basis, the human reality will no longer be defined by endless competition, tribalism, and war. There will no longer be a need for armies, borders, or nation-states. Moreover, the reallocation of resources away from armies and guns could be used toward the collective good and proper stewardship of the planet. Once human beings are liberated by science and empiricism, humankind can finally become united by global cooperation and a set of shared values that transcend religion, nationality, and capitalism.

How does an everyday parent refute this professorial paradise with an adequate response?

How do we flip our college-educated kids back to the idea that freedom from tyranny represents the highest level of utopia here on Earth? Unfortunately, the progressive worldview of human nature provides an easier path to inner peace and tranquility than the pessimistic alternative that comes with tolerating capitalism, guns, and inequality.

And today, we no longer have the greater platform with our kids and grandchildren. The days of ministers, priests, and parents dictating cultural norms in America are long over. The radical professors from the 1960s have gone mainstream, and today, they control nearly every facet of our culture.

If given a choice, I'd much rather live in the world of the college professors over that of the twentieth-century preachers. Like the seventy-two virgins awaiting the Muslim martyr, there is a future paradise of peace, fairness, and equality for those willing to follow Bernie Sanders or Alexandria Ocasio-Cortez.

But what happens to the West if universal peace and widespread harmony lie far beyond the reach of the human existence?

What will the future hold to the United States if there is no such earthly reality as universalism and global harmony?

While attending college for those three decades, I saw utopia painted out in many ways. And make no mistake—once an idealistic student finds a way to intellectualize the notion that human beings can set aside egotism and selfishness, there is no turning back.

If one buys into the intellectual narrative that human nature has yet another gear, it's easy to understand why the American founding (and the Israeli founding for that matter) are so problematic to the left. If human beings are capable of mass cooperation and equal outcomes, the Founders failed miserably as human beings. They used coercive tactics to dominate and eradicate other cultures.

And the villains weren't women; women were stuck at home with the kids.

No, the true villains were men—specifically, White men.

The progressives, the liberals, the social Democrats, the Marxists—whatever name you want to assign today—are not only split with the Republicans over important political issues;

both sides, in fact, have a much bigger problem. Every step forward for one represents an existential step backward to the other. Every new weapon system developed by Boeing or General Dynamics means a greater probability of peace to the traditionalist, and an unwarranted arms race to the progressive *do-gooder*. Every border wall that comes down represents global unification to the left and cultural fragmentation to the traditional right.

Facebook is another example that illustrates the philosophical debate of our time. To someone like Mark Zuckerberg, Facebook was the ultimate vehicle capable of steering humanity toward a greater level of understanding and global cooperation. To the human nature realist, however, it shouldn't have come as a big surprise that human beings with dubious intentions would also use social media platforms to spread hate, propaganda, and misinformation.

Make no mistake; it is difficult being on the pessimistic side of the human nature divide. Even when I had the facts on my side, I would still lose arguments to some professors. Here is another professorial diatribe that looked great on paper but not so great behind the scenes:

Professor to class:

Have any of you been following the debate about midnight basketball being rejected by the Republicans? I just can't understand Republicans. The legislators who oppose the idea of getting kids away from the drug dealers at night are the very same folks who will give tax breaks to the wealthy. Republicans will pay for more prisons, but they can't support a proactive program that attempts to keep at-risk kids off the streets at night.

When listening to the professor's argument at first glance, how could anyone oppose midnight basketball without being "mean-spirited" or "lacking empathy"?

Granted, midnight basketball did seem great on paper. Instead of hanging out on the streets late at night, troubled kids could be playing organized basketball. But around that time, the largest city in my state was a cesspool of corrupt bureaucrats and "pay to play" politicians. As the midnight basketball idea was gaining traction with the local media, I had a politically connected customer ask my company to do an evaluation of several dilapidated buildings in the downtown district. Sure enough, the buildings were run-down and had been abandoned for years. When I reported the poor findings back to the customer, he told me the scoop:

"If that midnight basketball bill passes, I have an 'in' with the politicians. If I can buy these buildings for a nickel on the dollar, put a little money into some repairs, and build a handful of gymnasiums, I'll get a long-term lease and be clearing big money from the basketball."

Fortunately, for the taxpayers, the bill went down in the state legislature. Had it passed, however, here's what would have happened:

My customer would have bought several old buildings in terrible shape and leased them back to the city for astronomical lease rates. Instead of a Bobby Knight running the program, it would have been Bobby, the-guy-who-knows-nothing-about-basketball, getting paid union wages to babysit a bunch of kids with poor adult supervision. And the politicians would have scored a *big* win-win. The program would have made for a great talking point during the next campaign. As to my prospective customer, he, his wife, and his kids would have sent out maximum campaign donations each year to keep the basketball leases in the family business for decades.

This story is a personal example of the bigger problem between the left and right. Even though I knew the midnight basketball scheme was a scam, I still couldn't beat the professor in this particular classroom debate.

He sounded so empathetic, and I seemed so *cold* and *racist*.

It's not that both sides don't see the same problems, they just see them in a completely different philosophical context.

With today's progressives giving disadvantaged Americans welfare is compassionate and allows human beings to get back onto their feet again. To us, giving people free stuff keeps them lazy and permanently dependent on government.

With open-ended immigration, the right knows open borders will lead to balkanization and democratic tensions. To the left, all human beings are members of the same global community and should be assisted with free health care, education, and governmental aid. To them, the United States has unlimited resources to bring in millions of unskilled refugees in the name of helping humanity.

The list goes on and on. With the 2020 Covid-19 virus outbreak, it won't be long before both sides march to their respective corners in the human nature divide. The Democrats will probably say the virus shows the importance of cooperating beyond borders and nation-states, while the Republicans will conclude America should never again find itself in the position of relying on other countries like China for medical supplies. And the latter would be most right. To a human nature realist, the coronavirus pandemic has revealed the basic truth that in an existential crisis, human beings will take care of their own before they help others. What "intellectual" could be naïve enough to assume China would ever place Americans ahead of their own citizens?

How could so many *smart people* in academia be so stupid about who we essentially are as living beings?

Beyond getting the human nature question wrong, the progressives also have a big problem with God. If human beings are perpetually flawed, who can be trusted to steer humanity to the utopia of universal outcomes and widespread harmony?

With today's left, the UN, the psychologists, and the progressive intellectuals are the moral authority for humankind. Whereas the traditionalist distrusts all human beings with arbitrary power, the Democrat Socialist has intellectualized the notion there is a benevolent group of human *saints* who have discovered the master plan to unite seven billion people.

But as the famed twentieth-century economist Milton Friedman once asked, "Just tell me where in the world you find these earthly angels who are going to organize society for us?" What human being can you trust over yourself, and perhaps a small number of friends and family, when all else fails?[vi]

- Dr. Anthony Fauci?
- Joe Biden?
- Barack Obama?
- Bernie Sanders?
- The UN Secretary-General?
- The Dalai Lama?

The traditionalist understands the answer to these rhetorical questions. If a person can count on one hand unconditional relationships based on friendship and love, he or she is very lucky. We don't elect superheroes to be public servants; we elect salesmen and sociopaths. Today, the talk is about Trump being a narcissist—as if Bill Clinton, Al Gore, and yes, Barack Obama, don't all fit the same psychological profile.

The Democrats are conflicted in ways that go well beyond politics. Unfortunately, the Republicans and libertarians also have their own philosophical problems.

How smart were the conservatives in believing a balkanized Iraq was somehow suited for a democracy? How did George W. Bush and his neocon advisors come to the brilliant conclusion that a myriad of ancient tribal cultures were ready to embark on the democratic path of one person, one vote?

In this toxic red and blue relationship, we must admit we get the human nature issue wrong too. To the libertarian purist on the right, the market has more standing than God. When a pharmaceutical company invents a billion-dollar blockbuster, forget about having an FDA approve the final product. Human beings can simply trust CEOs will do the right thing.

How misguided is this type of thinking? Didn't the United States already go down the path of unregulated capitalism in the last century?

Corporations will follow society to its lowest common denominator to maximize profits.

Putting absolute faith in the marketplace is no different than what the Democrats are doing in over-trusting central planners and career bureaucrats. It almost feels as if both sides are spinning their wheels in the philosophical abyss with no logical endpoint in sight. As with most divorces, both sides share culpability in a marriage gone awry. Both voting blocs can easily point fingers at each other's flaws to reinforce their own misguided beliefs.

Until we fix our own underlying problems, how can we step beyond a broken marriage with confidence and conviction? How will we win over millions of mass-movement converts if we are just as confused as our partner is?

Today, the worst aspects of Republican-sponsored big business and left-wing academia have combined to define who we are as a civilization. While big business works to build an algorithm that can anticipate consumer spending habits to the penny, the academics have strong-armed millions of voters into believing life can be *fair*.

The present-day combination of mass consumerism on the right and pseudo-intellectualism on the left may just explain why the United States needs to consider the radical idea of blowing everything up and starting over.

Saul Alinsky (1909-1972) was the master 1960s agitator who wrote the script on how to take power away from the "Haves" of society. It is no longer a secret Alinsky's book, *Rules for Radicals*, captured the imaginations of a young Barack Obama and Hillary Rodham.[vii]

Alinsky understood the hippie radical with long hair didn't represent the path of taking power away from the traditional *custodians* of society. Alinsky's script was essentially based on getting the hippie to the barber, buying him a nice suit, and then teaching him how to blend in with the people who would one day be overthrown. As Alinsky once opined:

> I feel confident that I could persuade a millionaire on Friday to subsidize a revolution on Saturday, out of which he would make a huge profit on Sunday, even though he was certain to be executed on Monday. [viii]

I think of this quote every time I see a mega millionaire hosting Democrat fundraisers at their mega beach houses. As Saul Alinsky alluded to, being rich and famous doesn't imply common sense. He knew once you learned someone else's rulebook, you could *club them over the head* into a state of submission. Alinsky understood no human institution could ever live up to its own set of standards.

By learning how to exploit the inconsistencies and hypocrisy of those who are the moral and political protectors of society, Saul Alinsky recognized a clever societal instigator could use clandestine manipulation, tactics of humiliation, and self-doubt to eventually overthrow an entire societal establishment.

One may think words don't matter much, but Saul Alinsky taught us words can have more impact than guns and money.

The 1960s radicals have figured out how to embarrass the traditional custodians of society, and they will shame any voice that dares to speak out against the present boundaries of political correctness. The academic elites have bypassed the First Amendment by stigmatizing much of the majority culture's normal thoughts and behaviors. The leftist fanatics have nearly won a stealth battle without having to fire a shot.

There are now millions of people who can't speak their minds because they have been marginalized by intellectual thought barriers and societal shaming.

Such tactics are not just happening at the University of Cal Berkley or Dartmouth. This type of one-sided intellectualism is occurring in the workplace, on TV, and in much of pop culture. Through the tactics of Saul Alinsky and others like him, today's traditionalist is sitting in a perpetual time-out chair. Worse, his critics have an open platform to disregard nearly every tradition associated with the belief America is an exceptional country.

If Alinsky was the field organizer of the left, Karl Marx (1818-1883) was the architect for today's Bernies and AOCs.

Marx witnessed the harsh working conditions and wage inequalities that arose during the initial stages of the Industrial Revolution in Great Britain.[ix] He concluded this type of workplace arrangement would open the doors to a future revolution between the workers and the capitalists. Marx wasn't an idiot. Even the most ardent defenders of capitalism should be able to admit in hindsight that anti-trust legislation and collective bargaining agreements from the last century were appropriate measures in finding a greater balance between workers and companies.

While Marx may have been correct with his initial diagnosis, he was inept in forecasting the future. Like today's Democrats and Republicans, Marx also got the human nature issue wrong.

There was never a glorious revolution that freed the proletariats from the bourgeoisie in Western Europe or in America.

With capitalism, the injustice is that a Mark Cuban can live a life of excess, while thousands of others are living on the streets.

With Marxism, injustice occurs when one human being who aspires to do great things is held in the same societal standing as someone who is motivated to do nothing.

When presented this choice, human beings will side with a wealthy Mark Cuban over the deadbeat brother-in-law who allows his wife to work two jobs while he plays video games all day.

By failing to realize the human existence is incompatible with universal equality, Marx's entire philosophical premise of a "workers' paradise" falls like a house of cards.

Unfortunately for humanity, millions of people have died trying to capture Marx's elusive utopia. Even worse, his false prophecy of a classless world is making a dramatic comeback in the Unites States. To the social science professors, the fifty-million deaths in Russia and China had nothing to do with Marxism.[x] No, the deaths happened because "the people in charge didn't do things the right way."

No economic system is perfect, but once the Marxists win over the masses, the storyline becomes very predictable:

- There is initial glee once the capitalist elites are strung up on poles.

- Shortly thereafter, economic shortages begin, private companies are nationalized, and inflation skyrockets.
- Political killings occur, and the elites flee the country.
- The strongman takes control under the guise of restoring social order.
- In the final chapter, there are no rich people left because everyone is poor—except for the dictator and his cronies.

I never understood how Karl Marx could be so wrong about his nineteenth-century, dire predictions yet be so in vogue with the artistic and intellectual minds of the last two centuries. Leftist diehards like Sean Penn and Michael Moore worship communist leaders in Latin American countries as if they are about to embark on a spiritual pilgrimage to the Holy Land.

There is a ubiquitous, Marxist bias found at today's universities obsessed with race, class, and gender. In the never-ending battle to find social justice and equality, society is in a zero-sum battle against the privileged, White male and his patriarchal traditions. Today's intellectuals have convinced millions of Westerners to believe traditional values are outdated, capitalism is evil, and human nature is ready to advance to another level.

This modern-day indoctrination explains why millions of Americans are more likely to self-identify with words like "privileged" than they are with words like "exceptional."

In Saul Alinsky fashion, the left has done a masterful job in shaming and victimizing half of the voting public into believing the US is a deeply flawed country.

The great philosophers who most influenced Western civilization didn't fantasize about perfecting and equalizing the human condition. Men like Plato and Aristotle saw balance and virtue as a means to offset a man's inherent flaws. In fact, our entire model of Western civilization is based on the premise that man is born deeply flawed.

- Incentivizing man to love and to forgive may have been the most transformative moral development in mankind.
- Harnessing egotistical impulse toward the creation of wealth may have set the stage for the most profound economic transformation in human history.
- Placing sovereignty into the hands of individuals, rather than a king or dictator, was the biggest political advancement for mankind.

Christianity, Adam Smith, and the brilliance of the eighteenth-century philosophers explain the intellectual foundation of the United States. Yet, all three of these tenets are under constant intellectual duress.

- God is dead again.
- Capitalism is destroying the planet.
- America is flawed because of White, male privilege.

College students are being taught the problem with human beings does not lie in their own inherent self-centeredness, laziness, and envy. No, the root of the *human being* problem lies in the *institutions* that made man this way.

It's not human nature that made us so nasty and selfish; it's religion and capitalism that have made us this way.

I acknowledge this type of philosophical jargon is boring to most people who live outside a college classroom.

But this is the type of lunacy that takes down civilizations.

What are the *two great intellectual myths* of the twenty-first century?

- *Globalism*: the notion human nature can be perfected to accommodate universal harmony.
- *Relativism*: the belief truth and morality are distributed equally in every culture.

What do these types of big words mean to us?

They mean *we* are the only thing standing in the way of a globalist tsunami that is almost certain to empower countries like China and Iran.

The true villains in our troubled marriage are those self-righteous intellectuals who have upended the legitimacy of any institution associated with the past. These academics and their minions in Hollywood are quietly tearing up traditional culture to pursue an intellectual utopia that will never exist.

Using Alinsky-type tactics, the radicals of today are handpicking the warts of the past to sow constant guilt, agitation, and division onto our democracy.

Some of the leftist agitators truly believe in a utopia of large-scale cooperation, borderless communities, and gender neutrality.

Others will jump on the Marxist ride with Machiavellian intentions, knowing the fall of traditional Whites will bring satisfaction and opportunity to their own dubious ambitions.

Who are the true buffoons in this stealth battle for power and dominance?

It is those progressive Whites who have fallen prey to the guilt and propaganda that individual liberty was built on the cheap, and people with white skin are somehow guilty and privileged because of circumstances that happened in another era that is long since over.

Who will be the big winner should White Americans be shamed into submission?

The Chinese Politburo.

The Chinese elites believe a market-based economy in conjunction with an autocratic controlled government will outlast the dysfunctional democracies in the US and Europe.

In the end, the winner of today's global debate will use some form of capitalism—that we can be practically certain of. The real question, however, is one of politics, power, and sovereignty.

Will power and sovereignty lie in the hands of individual human beings—the American way?

Or will absolute power lie in the hands of a Politburo—the Chinese way?

One must give the 1960s radicals their due. The academics stuck to their Marxist script with persistence and fervor, and today, they are within reach of overturning the most dominant power structure the world has ever known.

The ground zero in today's great twenty-first century divide begins at the universities and trickles down into every public school classroom. As a country, we allow future generations to be indoctrinated with such nonchalance, and then wonder how Bernie Sanders can attract millions of like-minded followers.

While it's easy to blame the front-line teachers for what is happening, the real problem begins with us. We are no longer involved with what really goes on in the public schools, nor did we ever question the social engineers who created the subject matter being taught to our children. We trusted the system because it mostly worked in the last century.

But today, the system is structurally broken beyond repair. Our schools have become indoctrination camps that prioritize globalism over Americanism, relativism over the Ten Commandments, and social justice over defending liberty.

Today, most American children will stumble with blank looks when asked, "Is America a great country?"[xi] And this is assuming they can find the United States on a map.

Our kids are also depressed and anxious, and they are taking their own lives in an unprecedented fashion.[xii]

Aren't human beings supposed to be happier in this era of modern psychology, do-gooder empathy, and global interconnectivity? Shouldn't our kids be smarter in this new world of technological advancement? It's now time to understand why the US system of education is the next battle line in our mass-movement discussion.

Chapter 3: Back to the Basics

A society with too few independent thinkers is vulnerable to control by opportunistic leaders. A society which wants to create and maintain a free and democratic social system must create responsible independence of thought amongst its young.

—*John Dewey*

The Founders understood a rigorous education was a prerequisite for maintaining democratic values. They knew a poorly informed voting populace would be ripe for manipulation, misrepresentation, and a likely return to autocratic rule.

In this present-day era of easy voting-by-mail, rampant fake news, and low-performing public schools, one can easily argue this democratic apocalypse may already be underway in the United States of America.

In the early days of the country, education consisted of children from all ages being under the control of one teacher. As the US continued to grow, schools mirrored the Industrial Era "assembly line" that inspired business titans like Henry Ford. Students were grouped by age and grade, standard curriculums were made, and tests were used to measure progress. Arguably, the system worked well for what was essentially a homogeneous society that required more factory workers than engineers.

By the latter part of the twentieth century, however, public education had become a federal behemoth, and politicians realized they could score political points by turning national news events into *helping the kids*. Each time there was a new fad in psychology or a momentary crisis in society, curriculums were changed to accommodate the social engineers and their friends in D.C.

When "self-esteem" was the buzzword of the 1990s, for instance, the bureaucrats declared *promoting positive self-esteem* should be the most essential job of the educator. For the next two decades, teachers were mandated to embrace modern psychology to make the child feel "whole."

And who were the recipients of the self-esteem movement?

You guessed it—the millennials. After years of undeserving praise and diminishing achievement, the experts began to change their tune about positive affirmation absent of real accomplishment. The elites realized an entire generation was prone to higher levels of "narcissism" and risk-averse behavior. Yes, the experts were wrong for decades, and today, millions of *adults* carry a level of self-importance that doesn't always match their contributions to society.

Can the millennials sue the psychologists and politicians for gross negligence? Can society go back in time and rewind millions of human minds?

No, there will be no do-overs with the seventy million voters who were taught positive self-esteem is more important than possessing the character and courage to accomplish great things.

In 2000, the Republicans entered the scene of public education. George W. Bush upped the ante by creating a massive new program that promised "No Child Left Behind."[xiii]

Billions of dollars later, the primary responsibility of the educator was to produce good test results. The test was the mechanism pushed by the Republican members in Congress to rationalize the massive federal dollars they had just piled onto the national debt—packaged as greater accountability in the classroom.

After Bush, Barack Obama came to the rescue with Race to the Top and Common Core.[xiv] Common Core is based on the bureaucratic notion every child in America has the same neurological hardwiring and level of parenting to learn at the same pace.

I sympathize with today's public school teachers. Not only do they have to accommodate bureaucrats, disconnected parents, and disrespectful students, they must also play the game of using a one-size-fits-all boilerplate with every student in America.

If the US was in a good place, teachers and doctors would share similar standing in society. But doctors don't belong to partisan unions that give millions of dollars to progressive politicians. Teachers can't have it both ways. The teaching profession can't be small, local, and nimble while being signatory members of a national union that is in near lockstep with the Democrats. At some point, teachers will have to look in the mirror and join our divorce discussion:

- Are most of today's teachers really educators?
- Or are many teachers merely pawns of the leftist fanatics?

A true educator understands not only where a child is in life, but more importantly, where he or she can go to next. The left loves to talk about empathy, the importance of education, and, of course, *the children*. But where is the empathy in advancing a fifth-grade child, who never learned how to subtract and multiply, over to a sixth-grade algebra class? Can any of us adults imagine what it must feel like to be completely clueless in a classroom and then be teased into submission by dozens of other adolescent children?

It sounds crazy, but this is what we are doing today with millions of young minds. The students are being run through the system like cars on an assembly line, and the adults wonder why so many of them are anxious, depressed, and hopeless.

Outside of a handful of students who can navigate the system, the United States is not inspiring its students to dream big and to love their country. Instead, the kids are placed into large buildings with hundreds of other immature minds and not enough adults with real moral authority. And rather than teaching its students how impactful the American founding was to all of humanity, our schools focus on the *bad* things the early settlers did to the slaves and the natives.

Forget the brutal atrocities the native tribes were doing to each other before the settlers arrived. Today, students are being taught the natives were all living together in universal peace and harmony until Christopher Columbus arrived.

Forget the fact that, prior to the Civil War, every other civilization had practiced some form of slavery.

Yet none of our forbearers ever went to war to end this abhorrent practice.

How many students are being taught this important distinction? How many of today's protesters realize over six hundred thousand Americans gave up their lives to end slavery?

America no longer educates its students with national pride, Judeo-Christian values, or rigorous academic inquiry. Whereas Chinese students are being taught to take pride in their communist and Confucian ancestry, American students are being taught to essentially hate who they are.

What does Black History Month imply to a typical Black, Brown, or White student in third grade? It means people with white skin were very bad.

Instead of teaching the Socratic method where every assumption of truth is treated with the utmost of academic scrutiny, today's students are indoctrinated with the politics of guilt, globalism, and privilege.

Our public schools represent the biggest civil rights injustice of our time.

To a casual observer with even a basic level of common sense, putting three special-need students into a mainstream classroom represents an impossible set of circumstances for most teachers. How can any educator focus on academic excellence when they have thirty-five kids in a classroom, six of whom are very bright, three of whom have a learning disability, fifteen who are average learners, and eleven who have little to no parental support at home?

This hypothetical example isn't a joke; it's a reality at nearly every public school in America. Just where do we find these superhero teachers who can obtain the best educational outcomes for dozens of students with completely different learning circumstances?

What are we doing to our kids with all these tests and the one-size-fits-all assembly line?

If a child has artistic abilities, there should exist the option of smaller schools that are 50 percent art and 50 percent everything else. If a child has attention problems, there should be a school that can slow down its assembly line roll and make sure fractions have sunk in before algebra starts. If a child comes from an emotionally deficient family, forget about Common Core, multiple-choice tests, and academic proficiency altogether. Start with breakfast, lunch, basic life skills, and a learning environment that is safe, consistent, and emotionally in tune with the horrible set of at-home circumstances faced by thousands of American children.

Beyond the outdated public school assembly lines, today's elites are now peddling a package of "free college for all." Should this *Santa Claus* proposition become an educational reality, the Democrats would enjoy a level of indoctrination in monopoly-like fashion. Think about this potential reality: what marketing agency wouldn't crave just a few hours of free, in-person exposure with its entire consumer base? Now imagine the college professors spending months and years with millions of young minds in an intimate classroom setting.

Over ninety percent of the professors support Democrats.[xv] The progressives and the academics love to talk about diversity—unless, of course, the subject is intellectual diversity. Just what kind of education can one receive when nearly every professor has the same political outlook on life?

While at the university, I would sometimes question why there was so little intellectual "diversity" in the classroom.

Me:

I don't understand how an institution can call itself a university when students are only allowed to talk one way out of fear of being shamed or beat-up. I think safe zones are a joke in an academic setting. To me, your approval of what I can say or not say as a White male is no different than what McCarthy was doing in the 1950s.

Professor's response:

I welcome vigorous debate in my classroom. But are you denying the historical fact that White males have enjoyed levels of privilege, power, and influence at the expense of nearly every other person sitting here in the classroom?

After this type of exchange, I would immediately try to get a read on the classroom. Nearly every time, I observed a similar result. Some of the White male students were energized by my little diatribe, but I would lose most of the Black, Brown, and female classmates to the professor.

The *disadvantaged* students seemed to accept the underlying logic that identity politics should take precedence over any other type of intellectual reasoning. Many of the students would become angry or dismissive of any sequence of logic that didn't begin and end with the intellectual premise that White males are simply too privileged to understand the full spectrum of a classroom debate.

The genius of today's Marxist ideology is that it pins the White-male antagonist into one corner of the room, while offering false hope and opportunity to the rest of the electorate.

In what is essentially another divide and conquer tactic used by today's social engineers, high school valedictorians are more likely to embrace "socialism" and "economic justice" over the previous belief the United States is an exceptional country.

In this brilliant reversal, the "smart" students are being taught to channel anger and hostility toward free markets and traditional values. "Free markets" and "traditional values" are, of course, the vehicles that foster *sexism, racism, corporate greed, destruction of the planet, and widespread discrimination.*

The "white blood cells" that once protected the concept of "American exceptionalism" are now attacking their original host in unrelenting fashion.[xvi]

As a country, the United States, and its traditions, are getting mercilessly attacked from both the inside and outside. Students are being taught that many of the world's problems exist because of the United States and its imperialistic past. International students from visiting countries like China and Saudi Arabia are attending our universities, hearing firsthand from the *American* professors *how bad the United States is.*

And the artists and celebrities are piling on by shouting out to the world the United States is a horrible country.

In previous centuries, Western elites understood the moral distinction between self-government and tyrannical government, socialism versus capitalism, and good versus evil. Just as previous intellectuals understood a vibrant democracy required its voters, in their totality, to be smarter than their elected elites.

Today, illusionists use words like "empathy" to rationalize trillions of dollars in national debt. Or they use words like "tribalism" to denounce those who reject open borders and globalism. Millions follow along, putting complete faith in government, academia, and the media.

Should the US remain on its present path of "educating" the best and the brightest to "despise American individualism" while dumbing down the rest of the electorate in dysfunctional public schools, we won't need a crystal ball to predict what will happen next.

The United States will remain on a path defined by two radically different *red* and *blue* Americas. One side of the marriage will be younger, Browner, and Blacker, while the other side will be older and Whiter. The former will likely follow the elites on a leftward march toward nanny-state governance, open borders, universal outcomes, and the politics of guilt, envy, and empathy. The latter will clamor for a fleeting past that is quickly moving beyond the horizon.

The "cancer" or "devil" in our marriage originated in academia and has since spread throughout every classroom in America. One would think students would be smarter in an era where tablets have replaced pencils and paper. Yet today, a student can graduate from college and not understand the most basic truths of the human existence.

How can a democracy sustain itself when its most educated people are too ignorant to understand the promise of *equality for all* will ultimately lead to *tyranny by a few*?

Nowhere is the failure of the educational establishment more apparent than in cities like Memphis, Milwaukee, and Detroit. In some majority-Black school districts, there exist schools where less than ten percent of the students are proficient in any one subject.[xvii] Assuming a democracy requires an educated citizenry, what is the answer in cities that have more homicides in a week than some countries have in a decade? Are White people to blame for poor-performing inner-city schools, incredible levels of urban violence, and racial tensions? Or do Blacks have to step up and fix their own problems?

We are officially moving into the dangerous waters of race in America.

In today's academic climate of relativeness, it is considered insensitive to talk negatively about other cultures. To the sympathetic Whites marching in the Black Lives Matter protests, inner-city dysfunction is to be blamed on systematic racism.

It is not the Blacks who should be blamed for their actions, but rather the Whites.

Our next step is to move the discussion over to a larger audience. Who are the various players in a bad marriage gone awry? What do we mean when we say "Whites," "Blacks," and "Browns"? What do these subgroups think of when they hear words like: mass movement and divorce?

We will begin answering this question by shifting our discussion to the *big elephant* in America's living room.

A bloody civil war couldn't right the big wrong of slavery. Trillions of dollars in governmental spending haven't overcome the "original sin." And the leftist agitators will continue to project the Black/White divide onto "racist holdouts" until time runs out.

Barack Obama likes to say, "It's time to have a real conversation about race in America."[xviii] But what's real to Obama may be much different than what's real to many other Americans.

It's now time to begin a real conversation about the legacies of slavery and what they mean to a marriage in great peril.

Chapter 4: The Original Sin

I have more respect for a man who lets me know where he stands, even if he's wrong, than the one who comes up like an angel and is nothing but a devil.

—*Malcolm X*

In 2018, the *Black* Republican nominee for the US Senate in Michigan, John James, garnered less than five percent of the Black vote in Detroit.[xix] James was a combat pilot and successful businessman, but was rejected by ninety-five percent of his own race.

John James was simply *too White* to win in Detroit.

Outside of the fringes, the real twenty-first-century battle with race has little to do with skin color. Today's racial battle is ultimately about culture, politics, and *power*. Blacks can call out Whites because Whites are *privileged*, but Whites can't critique Blacks because the former are *disadvantaged*.

This dynamic has scared the daylights out of not only most Whites, but also every public relations department in corporate America.

The antagonist in this book has a mostly white face. As with most divorces, there are others standing on the peripheral looking to take advantage of a divided marriage. I spent a lot of time up close and personal in inner-city schools and housing projects. As we shall soon discuss, there is more to the Black/White story than racist cops and discrimination in the workplace.

I'm not looking to pick unnecessary fights in this book, but there is no denying the symbiotic relationship between the Black voter and the White socialist.

Today, this quid pro quo alliance is stifling free speech and wreaking political havoc on our great country. Who would dare say anything bad about Black culture and not expect to be demonized as a racist? And who can take any pride in the founding of America without being privileged?

We have learned from Saul Alinsky that words can shape a powerful narrative. Today, it is a "no-no" for Whites to negatively critique other cultures, unless of course, they condemn their own culture. The do-gooders have created an entire nomenclature that incentivizes "good" thoughts while punishing "bad" thoughts.

Words like *racism*, *inclusion*, and *diversity* have the power to shape every aspect of our lives. If one does not fully embrace the idea of *inclusion*, being packaged to the masses as *diversity*, they are quickly tarred and feathered a *racist*.

As an American, I feel tremendous pride in knowing a handful of settlers were willing to risk everything to guarantee our freedoms today. Men like Franklin and Washington didn't *have* to do what they did in the late 1700s. By taking the American side in the Revolutionary War, Benjamin Franklin split his family in two.[xx] Thousands of others died to pursue the risky proposition that human beings should be able to control their own destiny.

Contrary to the sermons given at most universities, the *original sin* in America's founding had nothing to do with who could vote and who couldn't vote in 1787. Granting White males with property the right to vote was a radical departure from thousands of years of tyrants, kings, and despots with nearly unlimited power. Any twenty-first-century academic who is unwilling to acknowledge the historical significance of diminishing the arbitrary power of a king or a pope is a modern-day fool.

The true original sin of the founders was not reconciling slavery to Thomas Jefferson's notion: "All men are created equal." By allowing this distinction, Blacks were essentially *dehumanized* into property instead of being recognized as human beings.

Even though the Founding Fathers had game-changing ideas for humanity, I suspect many of them knew this monumental contradiction would come back to haunt the Republic for the ages. But they also understood the Southern delegates would never ratify the US Constitution if slavery was on the table. So, they kicked the can down the road. I understand Blacks have paid the biggest price in the greatest contradiction of our nation's history. But thousands of Whites paid the ultimate price during the Civil War. And here we are today—still trying to sort out a two-hundred-fifty-year-old mess.

In the entire realm of life, we are all God's children. All of us are small, replaceable, and mortal. But in the realm of how to live the most ideal life, we have choices as human beings.

And those choices matter in a democracy.

After spending years personally working in Black-majority housing complexes, I was shocked by the emotional, intellectual, and physical neglect so easily dismissed as normal parenting. The enabling Whites will predictably say bad parenting is found in every race. But I am confident these *social justice warriors* are not living in the same world many of our police officers call "work."

If today's empathetic Whites were actually living in the neighborhoods they claim to care so much about, there would probably be as much—if not more—anger directed at those bureaucrats who have spent decades defining compassion as placing millions of voters into a permanent cycle of dysfunction and dependency.

For years, I witnessed everyday dysfunction from mostly Black households that went beyond comprehension. Just as I witnessed poor-performing K-12 schools that would never be tolerated anywhere else in America. If you don't believe my observations, pay closer attention to the first ten minutes of the morning news. Go spend a week in an urban motel located just outside the downtown entertainment district in nearly any large American city.

Or simply look at the statistics.

Before the Great Society programs of the 1960s, 60 percent of Black parents were married.[xxi] Using recent data, *81* percent of Black children in cities like Detroit are born out of wedlock.[xxii] In some inner-city high schools, there exist entire graduating classes where not a single student is prepared to move onto college.[xxiii] Sure, there are some young men and women who can find personal success without a solid foundation of parenting and schooling, but these impressive human beings are outliers. Single-parent families are undeniably the biggest predictor of unwanted pregnancies, low wages, or imprisonment.[xxiv]

Even though Blacks make up only 13 percent of the US population, 41.6 percent of welfare recipients are Black.[xxv] In terms of prison incarceration, 34 percent of all inmates are Black.[xxvi] Between 1980 and 2008, Blacks committed more than 50 percent of all homicides in the US.[xxvii] And although this next statistic will never show up on the nightly news, *89 percent of all Black murder victims are killed by other Blacks!*[xxviii]

In cities like Chicago, *dozens* of Blacks are shot by each other every weekend. And some of the victims are innocent children. Where is the outrage when two or three children are caught in the crossfire of a weekend shooting spree?

Why does it seem like Black lives only matter when the perpetrator is White?

These are tough statistics for the White apologists to refute. How do the millennial protesters and their baby-boomer professors place so much blame onto *racist cops* when it is Blacks killing other Blacks in such an alarming fashion?

And at what point will the media begin telling *the other side of the story* of what it means to be Black in America?

In the aftermath of the 2020 police killings, corporations are stepping over themselves to change their hiring policies. Today, companies are doling out billions of dollars to advance the causes of social justice and diversity. But where do these corporations think they are going to find a stream of Black talent in communities with 70-80 percent out of wedlock rates?

One doesn't have to have a PhD to understand the reality that early childhood dynamics significantly influence a human being's ability to process cause and effect, language, attitude, and ethics. In what has essentially become a chicken-versus-the-egg question, are today's Blacks underrepresented in important levels of society because of systematic racism, or is their reduced standing better explained by a preponderance of unstable families and dysfunctional public schools?

Much of the Black identity is measured by other Blacks in how they interact with Whites. The power of Uncle Tom is alive and well. This nineteenth-century literary caricature continues to prevent many Blacks from embracing few aspects of White culture.[xxix]

Today, Uncle Tom is the mechanism that groups independent thinkers like Ben Carson and Clarence Thomas into the lexicon of house Negroes and sellouts. Any Black who finds personal success through the back channels of White culture understands the risks of being too aligned with the *master*.

Sadly, the small percentage of Blacks who find cultural, emotional, and political alignment with traditional Whites must watch their backs from every angle. These Americans still encounter pockets of ignorant Whites while also being shunned by much of their own race.

The perfect role model for Blacks *should* have been President Barack Obama. Unfortunately, Obama put politics and his agitating instincts ahead of having real discussions about race in America. Obama danced around the core issues of greater individual accountability, responsible parenting, and escaping the life-long dependency that seems to follow federal dollars and public housing complexes.

Before the COVID-19 pandemic, Trump had Blacks working in greater numbers than ever before,[xxx] but he still lost nearly 90 percent of their vote in 2020. If more Blacks were willing to move away from the do-gooder Whites at the voting booth, our problems could become much less complicated. If more Blacks were willing to spread their votes, hearts, and minds beyond a Democrat ideology that fosters permanent reliance to the state, traditional Whites and Browns would have greater empathy in helping Blacks with bad cops, workplace hiring, and shutting down terrible schools. If Blacks didn't have so many conflicts in finding self-reliance, more Whites and Browns would open *their* hearts to better understand the different reality that comes with being Black in America.

And if Blacks dealt with killer cops without looting and burning down buildings, they could expand grave instances of police injustice into a lasting movement that transcends skin color and political affiliation.

Unfortunately, the inherent contradiction of slavery with the Declaration of Independence is a structural fault line that has been manipulated by bad actors from every race. If a societal divorce were as easy as an individual breakup, Blacks and Whites would have parted ways centuries ago.

Since the messy aftermath of slavery and the horrendous Civil War, the US has taken awkward and ugly paths to correct its original sin. There was the view slavery was morally wrong, but society had to do everything possible to shield the White culture from a dysfunctional slave culture. This plan was accomplished with "three-fifths votes," "separate but equal," and "Jim Crow."

In the 1960s—and a hundred years removed from the Civil War—the Democrats upped the ante on assimilating Blacks and Whites.

Facing the political reality of 90 percent of the Black population being loyal to Lincoln's Republican Party, Lyndon Johnson dreamed of a "Great Society" that would eradicate poverty and get more Blacks into the mainstream of society. Rather than solving the Black/White divide through an aggressive cultural and racial showdown, the elite Whites decided to get Blacks into the game gradually, and they did so primarily through affirmative action initiatives, HUD housing placement, extending welfare policies, and pressuring their labor friends to open the doors of the union halls to more Blacks.

Fifty years later, the economic standing of Blacks remains largely unchanged.[xxxi] After trillions of dollars, an overwhelming majority of Blacks are still sitting on the backbenches of society.

As a former federal contractor, I personally witnessed how quotas end up playing out in the real world. Black community activists in cities like Detroit and Cleveland were always uneasy when a crew of Whites, *and Latinos*, would show up to perform construction work without majority-Black representation.

Contracts were thus mandated to demonstrate at least 50 percent of the workforce was Black. Companies that failed to validate their "participation rates" through certified payroll were forced to pay fines and penalties.

What was the most common result of the social engineers?

Most companies would factor the fines and penalties right into their overall bids. Companies knew how difficult it was to pull highly skilled workers off the street. Throw in the added employment requirements of passing a drug test and having a valid driver's license and it was nearly impossible to meet the quota guidelines.

The cities that needed the money the most, often wasted millions of dollars trying to promote *diversity*.

While there will be outliers who can overcome tremendous odds, society will never be able to buy the emotional stability and self-independence rooted in unconditional love and parental boundaries. The academics will, of course, continue to intellectualize and project Black dysfunction back onto Republicans, racist CEOs, and privileged Whites. And the apologetic Whites will line up in solidarity to show the world how empathetic they are.

To the social engineers, more money and greater tolerance are the keys to finally finding social justice and economic equality for Blacks.

Today, the Democrats want to double down on the failures of the 1960s Great Society with a new trillion-dollar behemoth called the *Green New Deal*.[xxxii] To put some perspective on this legislative initiative, groups like the American Action Forum have forecasted this proposed bill would cost anywhere from fifty-one to ninety-three trillion dollars, or six hundred thousand dollars per US household.[xxxiii]

The Whites who want to keep throwing money at the problem of race don't see, or simply refuse to see, the everyday dysfunction of a culture that desperately needs to try a different approach than spending trillions of dollars.

There is also a big disconnect occurring between the *empathetic Whites* from afar and those *real-world Whites* who witness the double standards in their everyday lives. Unfortunately, this divergence leads us to another unpleasant question with race:

When does simply being "*aware*" cross the line of being a "*racist*"?

Should human beings ignore the reality that walking around the wrong areas of most American cities is a bad idea, or should they keep their eyes wide open and hope everything will work out okay?

Am I racist in thinking 80 percent out-of-wedlock birth rates and poor-performing schools will keep most Blacks at the bottom rungs of society well into this century?

Am I racist for saying it is time for Blacks to finally get their act together with greater accountability?

Just how long was the affirmative action plan supposed to last? Fifty years? A hundred years? And what were the benchmarks to measure progress?

We know the answer to these questions: there were *never* any timetables or benchmarks. Today's Whites must keep paying an eighteenth-century tab that has no endpoint in sight.

In 1961, Martin Luther King Jr. said the following:

> Do you know that Negroes are 10 percent of the population in Saint Louis and are responsible for 58 percent of its crimes? We've got to face that. And we've got to do something about our moral standards... We know that there are many things wrong in the White world, but there are

many things wrong in the Black world, too. We can't keep on blaming the White man. There are things we must do for ourselves.[xxxiv]

This statement was made nearly sixty years ago. Why is there still so much dysfunction found in Black culture? Just how long do Whites have to stay in the penalty box for sins last committed 150 years ago? And when will enough Blacks be able to embrace self-government without the help of Whites?

I understand prejudice and discrimination are real—I'm not living in some kind of fantasy world where everything is perfect with White people. I have no doubt law-abiding Blacks carry a level of irrelevance most Whites simply can't understand. The Black twentieth century writer Ralph Ellison spoke of feeling "invisible" in a White-dominated world: *"I am invisible, understand, simply because people refuse to see me."*[xxxv]

Few Whites can sympathize with the everyday reality that comes with being marginalized to the point of feeling *irrelevant* as a human being. And most Whites can't comprehend the feeling that comes with being under constant suspicion. Imagine living in an everyday reality where a police officer is not viewed as a friendly protector, but rather a potential tyrant who has a license to kill.

Imagine walking into a bank, or any other place of business, and dealing with the unnecessary stares and the added suspicion.

Envision walking into a job interview, knowing the person conducting the interview has no intention of ever hiring a Black person.

And imagine being a parent, knowing your child is going to face a reality no other child in America will ever have to consider. How does a Black parent tell their child the United States is so great when America's most glaring imperfection is always in plain sight?

As with most bad marriages, Blacks and Whites have plenty of evidence to simply walk away from each other. Both groups continue walking on eggshells hoping one racially charged police encounter doesn't escalate into widespread civil unrest.

In my final years at the university, I was troubled by a trend that has since moved outside of the classroom. In the late 2000s, it was becoming commonplace for the professors to denounce White culture in an open forum. If this level of hatred was directed at any other demographic beyond Whites, professors would be fired, and universities would be in full damage-control mode. But just as Blacks understand the double standards that come with a job interview or an encounter with the police, traditional Whites understand the double standards that come with what to say or, more importantly, what *not* to say.

Blacks are attending college today in greater numbers.[xxxvi] The social science agitators are fanning Marxist tensions between Blacks and Whites because they view twenty-first-century Blacks as potential foot soldiers in that long-awaited revolution against the millionaires and billionaires. In an era when celebrities and athletes have a bigger platform than nearly anyone else in society, the social justice warriors at the universities have figured out that a Black athlete or entertainer who makes it big may become the perfect spokesperson to carry the Marxist fight into the living rooms of every American household.

Should my anecdotal observations from the classroom be correct, educated Blacks will become even more emboldened to aggressively reject the *evil* ways of White America.

Today, the term for such an awakening is referred to as "woke," and leftist movements like Black Lives Matter and Antifa have a much different motivation than what MLK Jr. preached in the 1960s. This potential set of circumstances, if not dealt with in an honest conversation today, could become the match that lights the divorce fuse of tomorrow.

We know the White apologists are very effective at using powerful slogans during Black History Month, but the great twenty-first-century myth is that White Democrat politicians have the best interests of Black Americans at hand.

Do the Democrats *really* care more about Black children, or do they care more about powerful teacher unions?

Do the Democrats *really* want more Blacks to be self-reliant, or do they want Blacks to remain a loyal voting bloc?

What the leftist elites truly want is to maximize their political power against traditional Whites. And the best way to accomplish this goal is to never let Black voters forget the sins of the past.

The White college students who feel so much pain and guilt at the Black Lives Matters protests don't seem to understand their "empathy and guilt" will only make the problem of race worse. Rather than focusing on stronger family structures, better schools, and having new discussions, the increased protests and lawlessness will only motivate both sides to distrust each other even more.

Martin Luther King Jr. also famously said:

> I have a dream that my four little children will one day live in a nation where they will not be judged by the color of their skin, but by the content of their character.[xxxvii]

A colorblind America will never occur if the US remains on its current path of guilt, fear, and identity politics.

Nor is there going to be a near-term reconciliation between Blacks and Whites under the precondition that Whites are *too privileged* to take part in a real discussion on race.

A colorblind society will be found when enough Whites, Blacks, and Browns look at each other for the first time and say, "Friend, we're in this together as Americans. Judge me by who I am as an individual, and let's put our country back together."

I recognize Blacks were invited to the original party with chains and shackles. But how much longer can this unfortunate past be leveraged before both sides simply give up on trying to understand one another?

How long will it take before more Blacks realize their biggest obstacle in America is not from those Whites who seem indifferent, but rather from those Whites who *seem to care so much*? And how much longer can today's Marxist social science professors be allowed to fan the flames of race before the US breaks up into two countries?

When can the United States begin a real conversation on race? When can we discard divisive words like Black, Brown, and White altogether? Why can't we all have real debates in the country that authored First Amendment rights? And most importantly, when can the Americans of today accomplish what the Founding Fathers couldn't do and what MLK Jr. hoped to do—that is, create a *new way* where individual character and merit become more important than skin color?

Beyond the Black and White divide, there are approximately eighty-five million *Brown* Americans trying to sort out the tension and acrimony.[xxxviii] Today, we use words like Hispanic, Asian American, and Pacific Islander with such ease and arrogance, as if someone of Mexican descent shares the same cultural values as someone of Dominican descent, or if someone of Chinese descent is somehow close in perspective to someone who is Japanese. This method of identity politics is not only absurd, it undermines the most fundamental American creed of E Pluribus Unum: (*Out of many, one.*)

What do Asian and Latino Americans think about all this crazy *marriage* and *divorce* talk?

Is the US a standard-bearer of individual freedom, or is American idealism simply a ruse only intended to benefit White males? Do older Whites hate foreign people who don't have white skin, or have the Democrats been successful in typecasting traditional Americans as mean-spirited and xenophobic?

I am convinced there will not be a successful mass-movement result without a cultural and political alignment between traditional-minded Whites and Latino and Asian Americans. Donald Trump should have understood this while he was president.

It is now time, however, to move beyond Trump, the Democrats, and the Republicans; it's time to begin a new and much needed discussion between Browns and Whites without any middlemen standing in the background.

Chapter 5: The Twenty-First-Century Swing Vote

The land belongs to people who work it with their own hands.

—*Emiliano Zapata*

My father was an example of the classic, twentieth-century immigrant story. He came to the US at the age of seventeen with ten dollars. He spoke zero English and spent his first years as a vagabond living in cheap motels and old trolley cars. Eventually, he would learn English, marry, have children, and start his own business. Later in life, I came to realize my father's biggest sense of accomplishment wasn't about making money or starting a company. His biggest source of pride, beyond family, came from knowing he had what it took to be an American.

We should be able to understand the twenty-first-century progressive mindset now. Today's do-gooders would explain with resounding conviction and empathy, how unfair it was that my dad had to sleep in abandoned railroad cars while some billionaire was living it up in Monte Carlo.

Whereas the traditionalist views the primary struggle in life as one against his own primitive ego, the progressive views struggle in the Marxist context of inequality and injustice. While my dad was sleeping in cheap motels in 1957, billionaires like Howard Hughes were sleeping with beautiful women in luxury Vegas penthouses. Using the logic of today's left, my dad should have first visited the Department of Social Services for an impressive array of governmental benefits before he got angry at Howard Hughes for having so much money.

One doesn't have to be a therapist to understand the negative energy associated with obsessing over the success of others. While society must be mindful when power and wealth are limited to only a handful of people, how did today's *intellectuals* arrive at the philosophical assumption that economic equality is more important than the ability to pursue happiness without having to worry about the watchful eyes of politburos and cartels?

I'm glad my dad didn't obsess over Howard Hughes's massive wealth differential. Like many rich people, Hughes wasn't all that happy. It takes a lot of energy to protect a vast fortune from predators and insincere friends. In 1976, the reclusive Hughes would die on a flight to Texas after a tragic battle with mental illness, loneliness, and malnutrition.[xxxix] Meanwhile, my mother and father had just bought a house with enough land to start a family business.

I live in a diverse metropolitan area and have friendships and business relationships with people from many different cultures. As a businessman and citizen, I don't care where someone was born. I just want to see newcomers contribute and have emotional buy-in with their new country. I don't know what the math is for bringing in either too many new people or not enough, but I support opening the doors to as many smart and hardworking people as possible.

We know why today's Democrats want to open the floodgates to "Brown" immigrants—they want the votes. The real prize lies in putting Texas into a perpetual "blue" column. This reversal would mean the end of traditional Whites having any further influence in American politics. The coastal

Democrats would finally escape the inconvenience of having to patronize the White working-class stiffs in the Rust Belt states.

Who are the approximately 85 million Americans that originated primarily from Latin America and Asia? Breaking this number down, 60 million Browns are Latinos, 20 million are Pacific Rim Asians, and 3.5 million are Muslims.[xl]

Let's take a closer look at the numbers and voting patterns of Browns, Blacks, and Whites in the 2020 presidential election:

2020 Presidential Vote Breakdown[xli] [xlii]

1. Brown (Latino): 66% for Biden, 32% for Trump

2. Brown (Pacific Rim Asian): 63% for Biden, 31% for Trump

3. Brown (Muslim): 69% for Biden, 17% for Trump

4. Black: 87% for Clinton, 12% for Trump

5. White: 57% for Trump, 42% for Biden

We will begin our *Brown* discussion with the approximately sixty million Latino Americans in the US.[xliii] Latinos will continue to grow in population due to higher birth rates and open-ended immigration policies. As they increase in population, and in votes, the push will be on by both political parties to expand their appeal to this culturally diverse group of Americans.

Should the Democrats win this battle, and the Latinos end up becoming the same predictable voting bloc as the Blacks, the GOP would find themselves in the same irrelevant status as they are in California today. Under this reshuffling of the Electoral College cards, the national Republicans would become dinosaurs stuck in a political no-man's land.

I have worked side by side with Mexican men whom I trust and respect at a family level. There should be little question Latinos will perform the manual labor most Whites and Blacks will avoid—even when the latter are offered higher wages. And contrary to President Trump's rhetoric, most foreign-born Latinos are lawful human beings who simply desire a better life.

It is true not all Latinos are like the men I crossed paths with inside the construction industry. There is no denying Mexico has big problems with gang violence and corruption; the cartels are omnipresent in many areas of Latin America. Mexico is ranked as one of the most dangerous countries in the world.[xliv]

Should the United States continue to turn a blind eye to border security, the level of violence and corruption found in Mexican cities like Tijuana and Juárez will find its way to US cities like Miami and Phoenix. Americans who visit Mexico, Brazil, or Columbia understand the power of cash and selective law enforcement. Turning a blind eye to corruption will kill any democracy, and tolerating corruption is the kryptonite that seems to follow the Latinos from every country.

The Latino people are not fools—they know their homelands are being overrun by the cartels and corrupt politicians. These Americans will support an aggressive US president who can properly distinguish between *the good and the bad* that countries like Mexico have to offer.[xlv]

Trump didn't have to humiliate an entire Latino-American population to win over more working-class Whites. This strategy was shortsighted and *wrong*. Latinos would have supported Donald Trump in greater numbers had his rhetoric been sophisticated enough to distinguish the *murderers and the rapists* from the millions of Latinos who are hardworking, socially conservative, and *good* human beings.[xlvi]

I am hoping today's undecided Latinos will look past Trump's rhetoric and understand the significant seat they hold at the table. If one is a Latino watching the White politicians banter back and forth, which group of Whites is most likely to lead America on the strongest path forward?

Is it those progressive Whites who believe girls are not really girls and boys are not really boys, or is it those traditional Whites who believe strong female and male identities are essential to parenting and protecting the future of their country?

Is it the Marxist path of Bernie Sanders and Alexandria Ocasio-Cortez or the freedom path of George Washington and Abraham Lincoln?

Do Latinos want to follow dependent Blacks and socialist Whites, or do they want to follow those Americans who believe in strong families, limited government, and protecting liberty from tyranny?

Contrary to what the media reports, most traditional Whites are *not* committing hate crimes.

What the traditionalist dislikes are unenforced laws, open borders, and federal immigration policies that don't consider a person's character, intentions, and skill sets. What traditional voters desire from other cultures, and countries, are productive and law-abiding human beings who will never allow cartels, autocrats, and tyrants to have more power than an individual sovereign.

How many people would invite a guest into their house who has a criminal record?

What previous civilization was able to remain cohesive and strong without enforcing its own laws, borders, and dominant cultural traits?

Traditional Whites need to start asking themselves some difficult questions as well.

There will not be a peaceful cross-border transfer of twelve million law-abiding Mexicans back to Mexico.[xlvii]

Nor is it in the best interest of our country to do so.

In what would represent a first mass-movement step, the traditionalist should begin the process of creating an effective immigration platform both sides can easily understand. Of course, there needs to be legal and regulated immigration. It would not be difficult to verify who is in the country illegally. A functional immigration policy would give "illegals" a grace period to report their standing in the US. Companies would be granted a similar period to E-Verify their workers. Those individuals who can demonstrate and document—via their employment records—a positive contribution to society, would be granted temporary visas from their countries of origin.

Any "illegal immigrants" with a gang affiliation and/or criminal record would be deported. And those who didn't voluntarily come forward would be deported once they have any encounter with law enforcement or any other governmental agency.

Allowing sanctuary cities and turning a blind eye to undocumented immigrants would be enforced as illegal acts on a federal basis. Eventual citizenship would require the ability to speak and write English and a proven track record of positive citizenry. In terms of building walls, the cost and the ability of deterring people from going over, around, or below any such barrier would have to be measured with results and not political rhetoric.

As we consider how to repair a very broken country with new alliances, the goal of the traditionalist would be to aggressively dispel the propaganda that "traditional Whites hate Latinos." In what may come as a surprise to the progressive elites, much of the working-class Latino population is not ready to jump into the same political relationship the Democrats have with Blacks.

In many cases, Latinos carry a level of hostility against Blacks that is rarely discussed at liberal think tanks. When I would mention this cultural friction to the college professors, this would be a common *academic* response:

Professor to class:

Well, that is understandable. Hispanics, like African Americans, are competing for the crumbs in a capitalistic system that favors Whites. This economic diversion results in primitive conflict and tribal behavior between the various Have-Not subgroups in American society.

I witnessed a different reality on the ground, however. Once our Latino employees saved twenty thousand dollars, they were out of the city and into the suburbs. These men and their families were in a race against time to get their kids away from the dysfunction associated with much of urban Black culture.

Like other traditional Americans, most Latinos will embrace a societal script centered around strong families and traditional social values. In a debate that goes back to Booker T. Washington and W.E.B. DuBois, many first- and second-generation Latinos are taking Washington's path. They are working hard at the blue-collar levels of society so they can send their kids off into a better life.

Contrary to what the progressive elites envision, aligning Latinos with traditional Whites is more doable than uniting millions of Blacks with the same. The real challenge is time. The college professors are already at work with their divide and conquer strategies. Just as Thomas Jefferson and George Washington are perceived to be devils by today's college-educated Blacks, Sam Houston and Davy Crockett will be the next dominoes to fall with college-educated Latinos.

If the professors can anger a new influx of younger Latino students over the annexation of Texas *and other acts of white imperialism*, there may be millions of additional Latino converts ready to join the Marxist cause of toppling *the imperialists*. And if the White traditionalists remain stuck on the bumbling path of being pigeonholed into an anti-Latino stance, they will end up playing right into the hands of these professors.

Beyond the Latinos, there is a smaller group of *Brown* Americans who found themselves in the news shortly after Trump was elected in 2016.

Studies show Muslims assimilate in America better than they do in Europe.[xlviii] And like Latinos, there is a wide dispersion of culture amongst the 1.8 billion Muslims worldwide.[xlix]

Islam, like Christianity during the Dark Ages, is trying to find itself in a world that has changed much since the fall of the Ottoman Empire. Ironically, Islam, Christianity, and Judaism are all bound by the Prophet Abraham and his two sons, Isaac and Ishmael.[l] These three religions originated from the same God. Yet millions of people have been killed in the name of religious purity.

The West hears about the Sunni-Shia split and the millions of deaths that resulted from their infighting. How did the Sunni-Shia split arise? After the Muslim Prophet Muhammad died, there was a dispute over who should be his rightful successor. Some followers felt the line of succession should have been based on blood (Shia), while others felt Muhammad's close confident, Abu Bakr, should have been the rightful successor (Sunni). These groups could not find alignment over this issue, and they have been fighting ever since.[li]

This is a true dilemma with all religions. What Muhammad accomplished in one lifetime was remarkable. Yet, once he perished, the inherent pettiness found in human nature soon reared its ugly head.

The problem in the Middle East is not Islam or Christianity or Judaism. These scripts have helped far more people than they've hurt. The real problem lies with the human beings who distort religion to align with their misguided impulses. And it doesn't take long for the fighting to begin once the divine founder exits a worldly existence.

Like Christianity and Judaism, Islam carries with it hope and ambiguity. Muhammad came from a merchant-class family, so it is possible Western-style capitalism and Islam are compatible.[lii] But many hurdles still remain between the two cultures. Islam allows private property ownership but has not fully reconciled the concept of charging interest (*riba*).[liii] It is difficult to embrace a twenty-first-century market economy when one must overcome the religious barrier of meeting a mortgage broker wearing a *niqab*.

Most troubling of all perhaps, the Qur'an has clearly defined rules about Islam coexisting with Christians and Jews. There is little gray area with Qur'anic scripture that instructs outsiders to either convert to Islam or pay a tax.[liv]

Islam, like Christianity during its dark spell, may require decades of self-introspection before it fully reconciles itself to the new realities of modernity. True, there are many great Muslims contributing to the success of the US today.

In addition, there is little downside in allowing more Westernized Muslims to immigrate to America.

But in this time of regional and religious uncertainty, why would the progressive elites be so anxious to import millions of uneducated refugees from war-torn countries like Syria?

Whereas many Muslim women in the Middle East are forced to cover their faces, teenage girls in the West find little dilemma in posting nude selfies on Instagram.

How do two such radically different cultures come together without first expecting conflict and chaos?

Shouldn't we get our own affairs in order as a country before we invite a guest who is battling its own set of problems?

When the standardized test scores for K-12 education come out, there is always one demographic that seems to stand out.

What do Southeast and Pacific Rim Asians bring to the United States? Low child out-of-wedlock rates, a strong work ethic, and a predisposition to do well in school. One would think these qualities would align with the Republican Party, but we know this is not the case today. The college professors are very good at reminding Asian Americans about xenophobic Whites and World War II internment camps.

There are, however, fault lines beginning to emerge between the Democrats and Asian Americans. The Democrat Socialists are nervous about the propensity of this demographic to earn big salaries. And the diversity police are uncomfortable with the disproportionate amount of classroom seats Asian students fill at many of our prestigious universities.

How long can the social engineers continue to discriminate against Asian Americans in college admissions?

How much longer can colleges like Harvard use "personality tests" to select its students?

The college admissions departments need to stop playing politically correct games. If one ethnic group occupies 75 percent of the student body at Harvard, God bless them!

It would mean other US students should study harder. Americans should be united by one set of rules and the pursuit of excellence.

Instead, the elites have pitted us all against each other. The United States is exceptional because it is the one country that has shown it can unite millions of human beings by ideas that transcend ethnic origin. Before the era of White guilt and progressive *empathy*, immigrants didn't come to the US for freebies. People like my parents came to the US because it was the one place they could pursue their full, God-given potential.

Why are we allowing the social engineers and race baiters to divide us by identity politics and double standards?

There are approximately 7.5 million citizens in Hong Kong who understand their days as a democracy are numbered. It may only be a matter of time before China wraps its dictatorial tentacles around this highly innovative group of human beings. *The Wall Street Journal* wrote that the United States should consider opening its doors to Hong Kong visa holders.[lv] According to WSJ sources, *67% of Hong Kong residents speak average, good, or very good English, and one in five adults planned to launch a business within the next three years.*[lvi] Why wouldn't Americans want to offer this type of guest permanent refuge in the greatest civilization in human history?

Our Hong Kong mass-migration plan is bold and destroys the progressive notion that traditional Americans are xenophobic. America will always be able to find a place for talented human beings who speak English. In addition, immigrants who live next door to tyrants and cartels are not easily fooled into believing the falsehood that humanity is on the cusp of embracing widespread harmony. Moreover, human beings who witness tyranny in their own backyards are less likely to be duped into picking central planners over freedom fighters.

If our country finds an opportunity to gain thousands of highly educated, hardworking, and entrepreneurial people who speak English, we should open our doors and say, "Welcome!"

Do the modern Greeks hide the Parthenon because their ancient rulers practiced pederasty? Do today's Italians talk about razing the Coliseum because slaves were fed to the lions?

No society can guarantee perfection or happiness to all. If traditional Americans can find a way to *divorce* their toxic partners, like-minded Blacks, Browns, and Whites can begin the first steps toward having a unified country. And should the United States rid itself of the intellectual Marxism and political correctness that festers in every corner of society, our country could find itself in the incredible position of attracting *millions* of talented and hardworking Latinos and Asians who are being chased away by bullies.

The United States could be on the brink of widespread civil unrest. In a revolutionary environment, Asians and Latinos could find themselves in the unbelievable position of deciding the final outcome in the United States of America. This type of prediction isn't based on conjecture; it's based on math.

If a traditionalist-led mass movement loses forty percent of Whites and ninety percent of Blacks, there is only one demographic left to decide which direction the marriage will take.

If we simplify our conversation to being on one of two teams—Team Red or Team Blue—it is hopefully becoming clear what the differences are between *each team*. In the context of a mass-movement strategy, traditional Americans need to create a different discussion than the narrative of racism and xenophobia. Expanding on a Hong Kong (and Taiwan) emigration plan would represent a good first step. In fact, this type of discussion should become an immediate priority.

Here at home, we need to begin a new conversation with common-sense Latinos, Muslims, Asians, and also, the seven million American Jews.[lvii] Each one of these groups is amazingly voting against the Republicans at a near 2-1 margin.

How long can this type of spread continue before the clock runs out on the original defenders of liberty and limited government?

Moving forward, there is another group voting Democrat at a 2-1 clip: our kids and grandkids.[lviii]

Millions of younger Whites believe open borders and universal outcomes are possible in the natural human order. To many millennial Whites, the word "socialism" brings with it a warm, fuzzy image of Uncle Bernie. Conversely, the word "capitalism" conjures up darkness and images of Dick Cheney.

Quite frankly, I don't know if today's millennials, in a majority capacity, have the fortitude to dig themselves out of a hole that began in the 1960s and proliferated after the radicals monopolized academia, Hollywood, and government.

On a per capita basis, studies can't show what many parents know in their gut: their kids were often raised in soft and confused environments with very little to believe in beyond saving the planet from capitalism and fighting against social injustice.

Today, there are millions of younger Whites destined for low-paying jobs, living at home with their parents, or living on the streets. I can't remember a time when there were so many twenty-something-year-old Whites holding cardboard signs at street intersections.

Look at the rates of working-age Whites who have given up on finding a job or the number of Whites who are on permanent disability in their twenties and thirties. Look at the suicide rates of these young Americans. And look at how many of them will die using hardcore drugs.

Younger Whites don't know if they are socialist or capitalist, innocent or guilty, or even male or female.

A majority of Generations Y and Z will not understand what it means to live life for a cause greater than trying to fight the confliction that comes with being *privileged*. This sociological reality brings us to a potential gut-wrenching decision. To rescue our kids from their handlers, we may first have to let them move out of the house without any contact or support from us. We may have to step back and allow them to move in with the wrong people before they figure out who truly has their best interests in mind.

Millions of younger Whites may have to discover the true meaning of life by living in the same neighborhoods as Colin Kaepernick, Michael Moore, and Alexandria Ocasio-Cortez.

The American dream doesn't have to be limited to student debt loans, privilege, and guilt. Just as we initiated a real conversation with Blacks and Browns, now is the time to begin a discussion of hope and redemption, with ourselves, our kids, and our grandkids.

Chapter 6: Divided and Conquered White

Those who see their lives as spoiled and wasted crave equality and fraternity more than they do freedom. If they clamor for freedom, it is but freedom to establish equality and uniformity.

—*Eric Hoffer*

Where do we start with "White" America?

Let us begin by putting ourselves in the mind of a *progressive intellectual.* Envision a global community without borders, guns, or inequality. How would we begin the process of constructing such a utopia? We would first seek to disregard every American tradition and begin from scratch. The United States and its *White* traditions represent the biggest impediment in finding global harmony and universal outcomes. Who has the most guns? The United States. Who has the most hegemony over the global community? The United States. Who perpetuates the greatest levels of inequality and social injustice? You guessed it: White people living in the US.

How would a modern-day Saul Alinsky sow doubt and confusion onto the dominant White culture? He would begin by indoctrinating their young and shaming the old into submission.

How would a leftist agitator break up traditional families? By marginalizing mothers and fathers and eliminating the lexicon of gender pronouns like Sir, Mrs., mom, dad, boy, and girl.

How would a George Soros globalist destroy traditional White influence? By dividing the citizenry into myriad factions and flooding the country with newcomers who aren't emotionally vested to the original founding principles of the US Constitution.

Whites across every spectrum of society have been divided and nearly conquered into a perpetual state of disrepair and division. Today, we are fighting against each other across nearly every demographic:

- Male versus female.
- Blue-collar versus white-collar.
- Young versus old.
- Rural versus urban.

Of all the battles going on within the various subgroups, we know the *real* enemy in the progressive plot is the toxic White male. In today's intellectual climate, it is difficult to believe a White male has a right to complain about anything:

- He has gained immense power and privilege by pillaging the resources of other cultures.
- His skin color is the same as every former president but one.
- He is the chairman on nearly every corporate board.

The sons and grandsons from the heroes of yesteryear face a new enemy who is far more lethal than an Adolf Hitler or Joseph Stalin. Instead of dying an immediate death from a bullet, the White male is at risk of dying a slow death from a disease that begins and ends with mere words. In today's hostile environment, he essentially has three choices:

- He can apologize for his previous privilege.
- He can become a Democrat.
- Or he can switch genders.

The social engineers are hard at work trying to teach school-aged boys how to become less aggressive and more tolerant. The broader goal is to shame the White male identity into not judging other cultures that are deemed to be disadvantaged. Making judgments about other cultures, of course, perpetuates racism, xenophobia, and global conflict.

The new rite of rigorous passage into manhood for twenty-first-century males isn't about transforming primitive impulse into a conscious state of courage, self-reliance, and love of country. Today's rite of passage is about learning how to discard the *nationalist, racist, and privileged* behaviors of the past. The role models for younger males are no longer policemen, firefighters, and Navy SEALs. These masculine heroes of the past are simply too toxic to be considered positive role models today.

My construction career began with men who defeated global tyrants and ended with adult boys who never learned that showing up on time, doing what you say you're going to do, and doing things you *don't want to do*, transform primitive male minds into reliable husbands, strong fathers, and the future guardians of liberty.

White males from previous eras built an exceptional civilization with a can-do spirit that arose from unprecedented levels of freedom and the individual toughness that came from taming a vast frontier. Even the most ardent feminists would have trouble denying the White males from yesteryear were the primary architects and builders of the freedoms we enjoy today. These men designed a blueprint to bring upon the greatest degree of science, medicine, architecture, and engineering the world had ever known.

Yet today, they can do nothing right. Thousands of former heroes are now looked down upon as disgraced "racists, misogynists, and colonialists."

I suspect many younger women are also witnessing the tragic fall of the confident White male. Trying to find a stable, mature, and masculine life partner is not an easy task in an environment where boys seem to remain boys well into adulthood. The experts say thirty is the new twenty. But I would suggest that both females and males in their twenties begin the marital lockdown process sooner rather than later.

Whether it is the immature male who sends *dick pics* before the first date, or the bipolar female with *daddy-daughter* issues, the talent pool of stable White men and women in the United States is shrinking fast.

Today is an exciting, yet stressful, time to be a woman in a global reality where brains and people skills matter more than physical strength. While there will still be male holdouts from a bygone era, there are tremendous opportunities for Western women that did not exist only two decades ago. But there is also great risk and unnecessary turbulence being fostered in a progressive environment that seeks to repair thousands of years of gender interaction in one quick and easy stroke.

Opening the doors to sexual equality between men and women, for instance, has changed the way young women think of themselves. In today's hypersexualized world, girls, even at an elementary school level, measure their identities against those famous females who are clever and beautiful enough to sexualize God-given talents into multimillion-dollar business models.

Before recent times, young women selected future mates based on the parameters set by the one male who loved them free from sexual intent: their dad. Today, however, many White adolescent women lack a strong, loving, and masculine paternal figure. As with most Black families, there is a good possibility the White father isn't up to the task of providing guidance, unconditional love, or even availability to his daughter(s). In this regard, the family structures of Blacks and Whites are converging in a new pop-culture climate that glorifies songs like WAP to every eleven-year-old girl in America.[1]

Can any of us contemplate being a teenage girl in this progressive era of fatherless homes and rampant sexual objectification of young women?

With the new norms in place, it will be a rough ride for those twenty-first-century females who don't possess the inner fortitude to keep up with the Kardashians. Instead of building a model of femininity from the inside looking out, the intellectuals and their cohorts in pop-culture are reconstructing a new female identity shaped by rappers and radical college professors.

Today, there are four-year college majors that can articulate—in extraneous detail—the origination of male dominance, how such dominance has led to unnecessary wars and inequality, and what must be done to rescue humanity from this evil. Women are being taught at the universities to defeat

---

[1] Cardi B, Featuring Megan Thee Stallion, "WAP" acronym for "Wet-Ass Pussy," Atlantic Records, August 2020, digital download, #1 Billboard Hot 100 songs.

men, and to even hate them, in the monumental Marxist struggle to find economic equality in the workplace.

I am not suggesting women have found societal equilibrium with men.

Today's women from *every ethnic origin* have the obvious right to continue fighting for greater rights. But the gender puzzle is more complicated than taking the earnings of every male and female, dividing by two, and then pitting today's future mothers and fathers against each other until the numbers align. The final result for many educated young women is the perception that true happiness can only be found when the glass ceiling is broken; as if spending an entire life climbing the corporate ladder has become more important than man, woman, and child being vested in a lifelong compact.

Rather than debating how today's men and women can find greater happiness and balance at home and at work, the intellectuals and their minions are diminishing the most important partnership in human history. White males are essentially being asked to hate who they are, and Western women are being reduced to *bitches*, *hoes*, and Marxist trailblazers.

Both are in desperate need of a mass movement that has the revolutionary power to unwind decades of guilt and indoctrination.

Beyond gender, there is also a big disconnect occurring between rural and urban Whites and blue- and white-collar Whites. As a former construction worker, I often left a jobsite and walked directly into a classroom environment. It was always fascinating going from a 40' ladder in thirty-five mph wind gusts to the theoretical setting of a progressive class.

It was at those moments, however, that I could best see the contempt and arrogance that some college-educated Americans have for those blue-collar Whites who vote for Republicans.

Disturbingly, Whites without college are far more likely to be unmarried than those who attended college.[lix] Neighborhoods that once housed future generals, CEOs, and presidents are under siege from opiates, depression, and suicide. Older blue-collar males are under attack for being toxic, unenlightened, and privileged, and their sons are stressed out trying to figure out why life seems to have so little meaning.

Contrary to what the academics believe, working-class Whites aren't voting Republican out of ignorance, hate, or globalization.

Working-class and rural Whites are desperate because they have lost their cultural standing in society. Before the crusade against traditional males, blue-collar men found pride in teaching younger males how to use tools and wit to accomplish difficult tasks. Until recently, there was equal standing in going to college, learning a skilled trade, or serving in the military. In centuries past, a white-collar engineer respected the blue-collar laborer even though both came from two completely different educational backgrounds. Importantly, both may have served in the military together.

Now, however, the distance and divide between blue- and white-collar Whites has little point of connection. Blue-collar parents are often looked down upon for being *deplorable* and *uneducated* not only by the leftist elites, but by their *enlightened and college-educated* children.[lx]

White-collar and urban Whites with college degrees are likely to view blue-collar and rural Whites as angry, sexist, and racist human beings who are stupid enough to vote for Republicans. Here's how a typical professor would intellectualize why blue-collar and rural Whites tend to vote for Republican candidates:

Professor #1 to students:

Twenty-first-century globalization and urbanization have adversely impacted rural and working-class White America. Technological advances and corporate offshoring have reduced the economic standing of lower-income Whites in a disproportionate manner. Working-class White people are losing out in a global economy, and there are political actors who have been successful in projecting such economic and demographic anxieties onto newly arrived immigrants.

Professor #2 to students:

The capitalists have cleverly created a political compact with economically challenged White people at the expense of African Americans. By demonizing people of color, they have created a cultural reality where fear and a perception of White privilege have united the White peasant with the White master. In this set of circumstances, lower income Whites are voting against their own economic self-interest.

Coming from a real blue-collar environment, I could easily understand how the professors were using academic nonsense to typecast working-class Republicans as racist, stupid, and xenophobic.

To many of my classmates, however, the above logic made perfect sense. Unlike most blue-collar Whites, younger, upper class Whites live a comfortable life in a globally connected world. Their helicopter parents made a good living, and today, the adult children are accustomed to nicer restaurants and traveling abroad.

If this demographic of younger Whites somehow escaped the liberal guilt trip while in college, their parents probably had the right connections to ensure a good career path to cities like San Francisco, Boston, or New York.

While in these "cool" cities, younger Whites with college degrees will see the best aspects of cultural diversity because everyone else around them is also smart and motivated. In cities like Austin and Seattle, the career paths of younger, urban Whites are in near-perfect alignment with the progressive message of embracing diversity and voting for Democrats.

This subculture of affluent, younger Whites often grew up in environments where individual identities were forged from carefully scripted parental plans that managed personal risk in fine detail. Big companies will do everything possible to recruit the brains of college-educated Whites through the proliferation of workplace fitness centers, impressive lunch menus, and bring-your-parents-to-work holidays. Corporate America wants the intellect and pedigree of the best Generations Y and Z have to offer, and they have found ways to merge personal insecurities into *socially responsible* work environments.

It is true these younger Americans are fueling a technological revolution that is no less important than what other Americans achieved in the past.

But unlike previous generations, this group remains well insulated from the worst aspects human nature has to offer. Younger, professional, urban Whites generally aren't exposed to the possibility of having a gun pointed to their head unless they make a wrong turn on their way home from a downtown Weezer concert. These educated and idealistic Whites have bought into the globalist platform that borders don't matter, and that all cultures are created equal.

Traditional White parents and grandparents are struggling to understand how a Bernie Sanders could have had so much appeal with their college-educated kids and grandkids. While older Whites can blame Sanders and his Marxist rhetoric, *we* should begin by pointing the finger at ourselves. We put our jobs and making money ahead of family time. We allowed the national debt to increase to unsustainable levels. We allowed the 1960s radicals easy access to our public schools, universities, and even our living rooms. We sat back and watched the cost of a degree triple, and we never questioned why the politicians ever got into the business of college loans in the first place.

Older, traditional Whites also share culpability in allowing the 2009-10 housing bubble to occur.

As fiscal conservatives, we quietly allowed the baby-boomer presidents to expand the federal government into the home mortgage business. When the government began competing against financial institutions for business, private banks found themselves pitted against easy loans and zero-down payments. But we played along with the pie-in-the-sky rhetoric anyway, believing Presidents Bill Clinton and George W. Bush when they said the federal government could build an "ownership" society.[lxi]

What was the result of the government distorting the residential real estate market?

A housing bubble that wiped away billions of dollars in personal net worth. Throw in the aftermaths of 9/11, the Great Recession, weak public schools, social media, and biased universities, and we can begin to understand why millennials are being drawn to a "Democrat Socialist" message that promises to project every defect from the past onto millionaires and billionaires.

Today, millennial, college-educated Whites are moving into higher positions on Wall Street and in Washington, D.C. They are seeking to fill the void, and perhaps lessen the guilt, that comes with being "privileged." As young adults, millennials in positions of power want to change the world in the image painted by their academic and pop culture role models. These Americans want to displace the guilt and apathy of being born White into a global cause that seeks harmony with other cultures and the planet.

I am respectfully asking White Generations Y and Z to truly contemplate both sides of the human nature question. Are my writings blinded by age, bias, and *privilege*, or am I forecasting the perfect storm for America and Western civilization? What will happen to your future if life is based on hard power, domination, and regeneration? How will your quality of life be impacted when older, traditional Americans die off and potential bad actors seek to fill the heavy hand of the twentieth-century cowboy? What will be your future fate if non-Whites eventually align together against the *privilege* that has been typecast onto all White people?

Thousands of White baby boomers retire in the US every day, and the federal debt is rapidly approaching thirty trillion dollars.[lxii] Who's going to be stuck with the final tab if the propaganda value of "White privilege" boomerangs back into the universally held belief that *privileged* Whites should pay back their own bill?

The older Whites won't be paying off the debt they made. Many of them will be dead before any difficult austerity measures have to be taken. The Blacks aren't going to pay the debt either because they don't have the money. And what about Browns—are millions of Latino and Asian Americans going to pony-up trillions of dollars in debt that was authored primarily by Whites?

History is littered with doom-and-gloom prophets who proved to be very wrong in their pessimistic assumptions about the youth of their era. Today, however, our country is in a philosophical no man's land between Karl Marx and Thomas Jefferson, and it won't matter that Trump is out of office—the turbulence, dysfunction, and national debt will continue to escalate in the United States.

When will *educated* Whites begin to realize they were *played* by many of their college professors?

Why does it seem like an imperfect Donald Trump is the last remaining White person willing to speak up against the intolerant cancel culture mobs?

I acknowledge the personal risks that come with talking this way. Communicating beyond the constraints of political correctness is a good way to be permanently labeled a Ku Klux Klan sympathizer or a Neo-Nazi convert.

But it is time to set aside the guilt by association. Whites are on the verge of being divided and conquered into a state of irrelevance.

I am suggesting *we* need to experience our own "woke" moment as the heirs to the greatest social compact ever made in human history. Our ancestors built something great, and we are allowing a tremendous civilization to rapidly decline with silence, guilt, and indifference.

How many thriving Black democracies exist in the world?

How many majority-Black cities in America have safe neighborhoods, high-quality schools, and balanced budgets?

How important were the Whites in assisting Pacific-Rim countries sprout their democratic roots? Not every culture has what it takes to defend liberty from tyranny. Before the era of cancel culture and privilege, Whites took pride in their democratic heritage. If Whites can't muster the confidence to begin having real discussions soon, they could lose everything. And when they fall, their democratic friends and allies will be in great jeopardy.

I want to return to our previous conversation about men and women. Earlier in this book, I painted a picture of my father as the perfect immigrant. Unfortunately, my dad didn't always come home at dinnertime. It wasn't until later I realized he sometimes missed dinner because he was out with a girlfriend. My mother was the true rock of the family, but like many women, she received too little credit. How does this happen, one may ask—how is it someone like my mother was relegated to second-tier status even though she was the backbone of the family?

If today's Whites don't seek real solutions to these types of difficult questions, there will be no sustainable mass movement occurring in the United States. Using my mother's example, White women will gravitate to the Marxists because having an "empathetic" plan is a better alternative than being clueless. Just as White Generations Y and Z will pick Black Lives Matter over their parents if the latter can't escape the guilt by association that comes with being *privileged*.

How can Whites find unity without joining right-wing hate groups?

How do today's millennials go about finding hope and happiness in a world that seems to have so little meaning?

How do blue- and white-collar Whites come to recognize they are both *equal* contributors to the future success of America?

And how do male and female Whites get past the Marxist nonsense that the ideal life can only be measured by fighting income inequality in the workplace?

By waking up before it is too late.

It's time for Whites to rediscover themselves before they lose their great country.

I don't see the dynamic of "White guilt" or "White privilege" changing without a completely different discussion on race. Whites can find their confidence again without being ignorant fools, but they need to understand they are at a defining moment in history. If they continue to run away from who they are in

90

such a reckless and guilty fashion, hostile actors will eventually seek to fill the void that comes from being a weak and divided people.

If we continue to allow our kids and grandkids to be so easily poisoned into hating who they are, who will lead the fight of being the most reliable defenders of freedom and democracy? American Blacks? American Browns?

Maybe in the future, but not today.

If Whites can't find the confidence to begin real conversations beyond the circular and nonsensical path that follows words like *racism, sexism, diversity, multiculturalism, and privilege*, they will eventually be conquered into submission.

Conversely, if Whites can find a way to harmonize their past and present into a future path of self-confidence and optimism, more Blacks and Browns will pick the freedom path of George Washington over the utopian path of Bernie Sanders.

We have learned from the Tea Party that traditional Whites can't fight back against leftist extremism by being afraid. It's time to change tactics. Let's stop with the incessant need to apologize for being *privileged and racist.*

Enough of the sensitivity and diversity workshops!

Let's open up a real dialogue that discusses the ramifications of either uniting as Americans *by character and culture* or breaking up the country by geography.

Should different conversations begin occurring in America, older Whites may risk their finances, and even their lives, if younger Whites, Browns, and Blacks find the conviction to speak out against relativism disguised as empathy, ignorance packaged as enlightenment, and Marxism promoted as virtue.

But if younger Whites stay guilt ridden, Blacks continue to knock down monuments, and Browns move closer to the progressive and Marxist Whites, older traditional Whites will simply fade away knowing the time of the optimistic American cowboy has passed.

We are getting closer to discussing mass-movement tactics and revolutionary theory. But we have one last fault line to visit. In 2015, there was a major battle decided without any formal debate.[lxiii]

Psychology tells us sexuality and gender are complex processes that play out in the minds of every human infant. Today, children in the West are being besieged with a cultural narrative that glorifies sexual and gender exploration at nearly every turn. Elementary-aged students are being taught that gender is a fluid choice, and anyone who disagrees is *homophobic*.

As the kids grow older, the new gender narrative of the twenty-first century will likely expand: *Are girls really girls and boys really boys, or have we all been playing in a rigged game where the human beings with penises created a set of patriarchal rules intended to dominate the human beings with vaginas?*

This type of intellectual lunacy is already playing out at our universities. If one believes men and women are inherently different and children benefit from such biological and cultural differences, where does the traditionalist go in today's world of gender-neutral pronouns?

Republicans were nowhere to be found when this battle was being waged. In another brilliant overnight reversal, unbridled sexual exploration has become the new norm, and those who question the new rules have become the patient with a diagnosable disorder.

While many Americans have concluded the battle with gender and sexuality is over, the opposite may just be true. The case on gender and sexuality needs to be reopened before the divorce proceedings begin.

Chapter 7: The New Gender Galaxy

Either you are homophobic, or you are a human—you cannot be both.

—*Abhijit Naskar*

Anthropology tells us men were hunters and women were gatherers for thousands of years. Males were physically stronger in a world that favored muscle over brains. Men fought in wars, so boys were trained to be warriors and hunters. Human infants required nurturing to offset the incredible burden that comes with a rational mind in an unexplainable world. The most logical choice for this important role was the biological mother who was one with the child for nine months.

The best choice to be the physical protector of the child was a strong male with DNA connection to the child. A social compact was thus made: females provided emotional security to their children and males provided physical security.

Today, the leftist radicals are in a race against time to overcome White-male dominance at every level of society. Academics have reached the conclusion that gender is merely a state of consciousness manipulated by patriarchal traditions. The LGBTQ community has convinced millions of us to believe traditional marriage and gender patterns are outdated and discriminatory. And the millennials are all-in with this new societal arrangement. Nowadays, if a twenty-two-year-old guy doesn't have what it takes to have sex with a girl, he can simply jump into bed with his bigender roommate.

There are dozens of gender and sexual orientation possibilities up for consideration today; how does the traditionalist make sense out of the fact another gender galaxy was recently discovered?

Let's take a look at some of the new human identities that make up our twenty-first-century gender reality:

- Agender: A person with little or no connection to a specific gender.
- Androgynous: A gender expression with both elements of masculinity and femininity.
- Bigender: A person who fluctuates between both female and male identities.
- Bisexual: A person who is physically, emotionally, and/or sexually attracted to both men and women.
- Crossdresser: A person who dresses and behaves in a way characteristic of the opposite sex.
- Gender Fluid: A person whose daily feelings fluctuate between a man and a woman.
- Gender Variant: A person who does not conform to the gender-based expectations of society.
- Intersex: A term for people born with a combination of female and male physical traits.
- Metrosexual: A term for a man with a strong aesthetic sense beyond the cultural norms.
- Pansexual: A person who experiences sexual, romantic, and/or physical attraction to all gender identities.

- Skoliosexual: A person who is primarily attracted sexually, romantically, and/or emotionally to some genderqueer, transgender, and/or non-binary people.
- Transgender: A person whose gender identity and/or gender expression differs from what is typically associated with the sex they were assigned at birth.[lxiv]

The new gender definitions are changing in exponential fashion. We now live in a world where it is socially acceptable to believe human beings are biologically predisposed to be male, female, or otherwise. We also live in a culture where previously accepted norms of sexuality and gender are reversing at a rapid pace.

An overwhelming majority of Americans have come to accept new gender definitions in ways that would have been unimaginable only twenty years ago.

In writing this book, I had friends and colleagues advise me to leave the issue of gender and sexuality out of the divorce discussion. Here were some typical comments from people whom I respect very much:

- "The real culprit in the debate is Marxism and one-sided intellectualism."
- "People may be born gay. I'd rather have two loving gay parents than two crackhead heterosexual parents."
- "By targeting the issue of gender and sexual orientation, you're going to lose every American under the age of thirty-five."

In contemplating how the United States could possibly move forward as a country, I just couldn't find a way to reconcile the notion that our human existence is based on dozens of gender variations. Nor could I envision a civilization achieving long-term success without being centered around the commonsense notion that a social compact between a mother, father, and child should be the most sacred institution of all.

The gender and sexuality debate of today is a true societal dilemma that goes beyond the US. The Chinese and Russians seem to understand the potential risks associated with moving too fast on longstanding norms that have been a staple of the civilized world for thousands of years.[lxv] [lxvi] I'm not sure how long countries like China and Russia will be able to stall the clock on gender expansion, but they are treating the issue with patience and the power of the state.

In a better set of circumstances, Americans would also be sitting back and watching how the new sexual norms play out in other Western democracies that pride themselves on "gender tolerance." Like the multiculturalism experiment occurring in Europe, we could have easily stood back and watched how the new gender rules ended up resulting in cities like London and Paris.

But it is too late to take such a stance now. Like Europe, we are now all-in with the new progressive definitions of gender, sexuality, and marriage.

In a 2015, 5-4 decision, the US Supreme Court ruled in favor of gay marriage.[lxvii] While thousands of gay Americans wept in joy, Chief Justice Roberts wrote in dissent, "The court invalidates the marriage laws of more than half of the states and orders the transformation of a social institution that has formed the basis of human society for millennia, for the Kalahari Bushmen and the Han Chinese, the Carthaginians and the Aztecs...Just who do we think we are?"[lxviii]

So, here we are again, peeling back the sensitive layers of a controversial topic that should have occurred well before the Supreme Court decision came out. This lack of public debate occurs because today's intellectuals will destroy anyone who stands in the way of *liberating* groups that were oppressed by the discriminatory traditions of the past.

Taking a step back to analyze the importance of the traditional male and female identity to Western society was never considered, nor was having a rigorous debate about the true origins of sexuality and gender. Is sexuality and gender determined before birth, or are these factors largely determined by environmental circumstances? And why does this matter to society?

If gender and sexual preference are determined before birth, why does *30 percent* of Generation Z in Great Britain today identify as something other than heterosexual?[lxix]

Sure, human beings were stuck in the closet before recent times, but the closet was never this big. Something else must be going on beyond genetic variance.

Sigmund Freud hypothesized psychosexual development begins in the early stages of childhood. Whether one is reading Freud or speaking to the parent of a *young* toddler, it is mind-numbing observing three-year-old children displaying strong, sexual impulses at such a young age. There must be a complex process on gender and sexuality that takes place in the early stages of human life.

It is also beyond comprehension trying to understand why deviant adults are sexually attracted to young children. Unlike other mammals, human beings have no biological disposition to bear offspring at five years of age. Yet, beyond the realms of our everyday existence lies a world of sexual perversion that is profoundly heartbreaking.

The progressives claim to represent *forward thinking*, but what Miley Cyrus and Cardi B consider to be new and risqué today was tried ten times over two thousand years ago. I admit, the origin of gender and sexuality is complex, but this isn't a situation without historical context. After the Greeks and early

Romans fell, every other major civilization tabooed the idea of homosexuality:

- the Hindus
- the Buddhists
- the Jews
- the Christians
- and the Muslims.[lxx]

Why did these cultures place so much emphasis on clarifying two distinct genders?

The *Diagnostic and Statistical Manual of Mental Disorders* spent decades trying to walk the line of whether homosexuality was a disorder or a normal condition that simply required self-acceptance. It seems to make anecdotal sense that some human beings are born with a predisposition to be gay. But it is also a historical fact that gender and sexuality can be influenced by culture.

The predominance of homosexuality in ancient Greece and Rome didn't coincide with an escalation in genetic variance; it happened on a widespread basis because the practice was accepted and promoted as a cultural norm.[lxxi] Human infants do not enter the world with a cognitive understanding of their own gender. Is it plausible early childhood dynamics steer infants and toddlers into alignment with their physiological bodies? If this theory is correct, it may explain why people feel like they were "born gay." If gender formation occurs in early childhood, no person is going to remember that exact moment in time when they *became* a *boy, girl, or other.*

The distinction of being "born gay" or "made gay" is really not our issue.

Rather, the bold and brazen attempt to move from the single issue of gay marriage in 2015 to a complete redefinition of gender and sexuality six years later is too much, too fast. Why is the West so fixated on prioritizing gender expansion over building a stronger compact between a male, female, and their offspring? Is there a special bond that exists between a father and daughter? Does it make sense that boys benefit from having a strong male role model at home? Do males benefit emotionally by having the unconditional love of their mom? And do girls measure themselves against a strong and feministic role model at home and in life?

I understand the everyday reality that no family is perfect. History is filled with examples of happy, high-achieving people who never met their biological parents. But we're not talking about individual circumstances. We're looking at a myriad of complex sociological arrangements that impact millions of human beings.

Any society that diminishes the institution of marriage between a man and woman does so at its own risk. More importantly, at what point will the expanding gender list stop?

The LGBTQ community simply overplayed their hand. They got their foot in the door and knocked down the entire house. They have framed the debate on gender as an open-and-shut case, and anyone who disagrees with the new norms is labeled as mean-spirited and homophobic.

Where does the list of genders and sexual preferences go from here? Once it becomes culturally acceptable for the gender-fluid stepfather to go upstairs for a rendezvous with his transgender stepdaughter, what mere mortal will have the power to dig society out of such a hole?

Should five-year-old children be forced to think about dozens of gender choices in kindergarten?

Should ten-year-old kids be able to demand *sex-change* surgeries?

The left loves to talk about human rights, but what rights does an elementary-aged child have if they are constantly inundated with an aggressive LGBTQ agenda?

Will relaxed standards regarding gender and sexuality diminish the Judeo-Christian covenant between spouses, parents, and children?

Will the new and expansive norms on sex and gender reduce the incentive for men and women to remain monogamous during child-rearing years?

Unfortunately, these types of debates never occurred either. The present-day phenomenon of the elites being "on the right side of history" has upended any tradition associated with making two genders and traditional marriage the primary staple of Western society. By taking the genie of sexuality and gender out of the bottle with so little debate, five Supreme Court justices have essentially placed the aggressive interests of a small and vocal minority ahead of millions of other citizens. And no one can suggest otherwise without receiving death threats.

Where were the Republicans when the debate on gender and sexuality began? This is the political party that supposedly stands for traditional gender definitions and two-parent families. Instead of fighting back against the radical gays and their friends in Hollywood, the Republicans stood down and allowed longstanding attitudes on gender and sexuality to change without a fight.

Hollywood first opened the curtain with Brokeback Mountain in 2005.[lxxii] The twentieth-century preachers warned breaking traditional taboos associated with sex and gender could open the door to a whole different set of unintended consequences. I'm not trying to advance the idea that sexual purity will ever exist with human beings. Any time someone begins to lecture others on sex and marriage, a hidden skeleton always seems to find its way to the surface. Rather, I am suggesting Americans should have exercised great caution before they were bullied into reversing two thousand years of tradition.

There are simply those conflicts in an advanced society that can't be easily remedied. It is at those moments in a democracy the citizens should be the final arbiter of truth and justice. Complex issues like gender and marriage should have been made by us and not the elites.

When society tells its children it is acceptable to become one of a hundred different genders, we are essentially playing Russian roulette with an entire civilization. We are asking immature minds to answer questions the adults haven't figured out yet.

I will never judge a human being for being gay. But just as the *LGBTQ+* community is asking for *tolerance*, why can't the opinions of other viewpoints be tolerated?

How hateful and wrong is it to suggest younger children shouldn't be burdened with complex gender choices so early in life?

And why would the most successful democracy in the history of the world change its most important institution without an open and fair trial?

Hopefully, we are beginning to understand the answers to these types of questions. We are living in an era of leftist insanity. The *silent majority* in the United States is too afraid to offend their hostile partner(s) on not only the issue of gender, but every other societal fault line.

As Americans, we are reliving the crazed era of McCarthyism all over again.

What today's thought police are doing with free speech is not unlike what the Politburo is doing in China. Or what the Ayatollahs are doing in Iran. Or what Putin is doing in Russia. It's time to consider a different strategy than that of the Tea Party. It's time to up the ante and force a real discussion with mass-movement implications.

Chapter 8: The Good, the Bad, and the Ugly

A society that puts equality...ahead of freedom will end up with neither.

—*Milton Friedman*

No mainstream academic or recognized media personality can expose the leftist radicals without secretly pursuing a reputational death wish. The moment any "established expert" tried to write that a trans female should never be allowed to compete in a women's sporting event, an entire career would be destroyed with one stroke of the pen.

I personally witnessed the radicalization process evolve over three decades at the university. We're no longer talking about a handful of 1960s hippies reading Marx and Durkheim in rundown apartment flats in Berkley. We are talking about nearly half of the electorate believing human nature is malleable, communism is a potential virtue, and universal equality should be prioritized over the securement of individual rights.

In hindsight, the biggest mistake of the traditionalist was allowing the Marxists such easy access into government and academia. The "swamp" has grown beyond control, and even those insiders with common sense are often powerless to take on the leftist dragon who sits beside them.

During the heyday of McCarthyism in the early- to mid-1950s, Republican Senator Joseph McCarthy, and others like him, had the power to destroy reputations and careers. Like all opportunists, McCarthy was able to use soft truths to expand his power to every corner of society. Back then, communist sympathizers, homosexuals, and Blacks were in the crosshairs of men like Joseph McCarthy and J. Edgar Hoover.[lxxiii][lxxiv]

In 1954, however, the dominoes began to fall the wrong way for Senator McCarthy. Joe overplayed his hand, and the public witnessed an *emperor has no clothes* moment in US politics.[lxxv] After an army hearing, McCarthy was exposed as an empty suit who pushed paranoia to consolidate political power. He died three years later at the age of forty-eight from alcoholism and an apparent morphine addiction.[lxxvi]

In his last years in the US Senate, colleagues shunned him, and the media ignored him. When he spoke on the Senate floor at the end of his tenure, many of his colleagues would stand up and exit the chamber.[lxxvii] This once-formidable man with near absolute power in Washington D.C. had been exposed as a fraud.

I'm not sure whether there is enough time to experience a McCarthy epiphany again in American politics. McCarthy was essentially a one-man band. Today, there are millions of *social justice* converts with very little to lose in life. They are committed to the cause, and probably won't go away without being forced to leave.

Thomas Jefferson wrote in 1787, "The people cannot be all, and always, well informed. The part which is wrong will be discontented in proportion to the importance of the facts they misconceive; if they remain quiet under such misconceptions it is the lethargy, the forerunner of death to the public liberty...And what country can preserve it's liberties if their rulers are not warned from time to time that their people preserve the spirit of resistance? The tree of liberty must be refreshed..."

According to Jefferson, it shouldn't come as a big surprise the United States is so divided today. If we weren't fighting over social and economic injustice, we'd probably be wasting trillions of dollars trying to find a unicorn.

This may simply be who we are as human beings. Powerful civilizations always seem to rise and decline in the natural order of life through decadence, complacency, and ignorance. The question we must ask ourselves today is how long do we want to allow the crazies to have an open and one-sided microphone before we decide to fight back?

America is not destined to follow the same civilizational path of ruin as Rome or Greece. We understand the historical mistakes of the ancients. We have the power of mass communication to discredit the Joseph McCarthys of our era with a simple social media campaign.

All we need is to find the right set of mass-movement trigger(s), and we can set into motion an incredible series of history-making events. Just as the progressives are energized with the Black Lives Matter protests today, the traditionalists have the potential to create a level of excitement that could make an Occupy Wall Street rally look like child's play.

Aside from a spontaneous set of revolutionary circumstances occurring without warning, I envision five *divorce* scenarios with the possibility of overlap. Although not sexy in nature, there is the chance a new political party and platform could end today's stalemate without the ugliness of a *bad divorce*.

As the Democrats and Republicans both wallow in dysfunction, there may be an opportunity for the party that can reinvent itself with a transformative, twenty-first-century platform. Under this type of mass-movement playbook, traditional voters would demand a new movement that has broader appeal to the entire electorate. The goal with this plan would be to avoid a messy breakup by taking the fuel out of the fire that keeps Marxism alive—class warfare and inequality. In creating a new movement in American politics, we would seek to diminish the power of the intellectual and artist classes by making ourselves relevant again in a majority capacity.

This mass-movement strategy would represent a complete overhaul of the GOP with new faces, new ideas, and possibly a new name. If we think about it, the Republican Party has already been taken over by Trump.

Why not codify Trump's political instincts into an official Republican platform?

My emotional attachment to the GOP is simply gone. Republicans have been traveling down a death spiral since Ronald Reagan left office. When a businessman with zero political experience can walk onto the stage from his private jet and defeat the entire Republican establishment, there is a big underlying problem within the overall structure of the organization.

In today's world, what does it even mean to say, "I'm a Republican"?

I have no idea what George W. Bush and John Kasich stand for other than being stooges who are easily manipulated by the tactics of Saul Alinsky and Karl Marx. The Republican establishment figureheads stand together with inflexible pride as they get attacked aimlessly by an asymmetrical enemy. They are impotent to fight back because they refuse to set aside the fond memories from a distant past.

These twentieth-century dinosaurs still have not figured out that Trump's election victory in 2016 was a rallying cry to blow up the entire Republican establishment.

The second divorce path is where things become more complicated. Let's assume the tension and acrimony continues. Maybe our problems escalate in ways that can't be anticipated yet. Should the US follow on its current path of dysfunction and debt, reasonable people from both sides will probably say, "Our democracy is broken; we need to try something radically different."

Our second divorce scenario is based on the notion of bringing the Republicans and Democrats to the table to discuss how to best separate from each other. This option is based on the idea of holding a constitutional convention to informally outline the ramifications associated with a geographical breakup of the country.

Under this strategy, a group of delegates would essentially present a "two America" plan to over three hundred million people, outlining the logistical, military, geographical, monetary, and political ramifications of a geographical split.

The British have shown us complex breakups can be negotiated in the modern world. None of us want to see the United States break into two countries, but what other choice(s) does the traditionalist have if absentee ballots and voting-by-mail schemes create an impenetrable *blue* wall?

Moreover, what choices will both sides have if today's dysfunction continues to escalate beyond control?

The third and fourth divorce paths are where things get even more dangerous. Without the advantage of hindsight, I imagine two specific scenarios: Trump is in *or* out, but the leftist radicals are still the primary drivers of our culture and politics. These two paths would represent a political environment where the dysfunction in the marriage grows, and neither side is willing to budge.

Assuming Trump remains on the national scene, we would essentially provide a revolutionary road map to an ex-president.

Should Trump depart from politics, we would provide "traditional agitators" a revolutionary manifesto that uses Saul

Alinsky-type tactics to radically challenge academia and the media.

The fifth divorce scenario could end up being the most likely of all. When our debt and democratic paralysis reaches a breaking point, no president will have the ability to cut spending and/or raise taxes enough without facing a revolt from the voters.

Our final divorce possibility, therefore, assumes millions of us may one day demand a "temporary dictator" to radically overhaul what has become a broken democracy. Under this scenario, the *dictator* would have arbitrary power to fix the hot mess that we today call the United States.

Beyond the tensions playing out at home, there is a stealth global contest that will impact billions of people before this century ends.

China understands a pure Marxist economy will never generate the wealth and innovation that comes with capitalism. Only those fools in Western academia would believe otherwise.

In this era of pseudo intellectualism and fake news, we are too blind to realize China is copying *our* proven playbook—at the very same time *we* are considering their failed Marxist policies from the past century.

After centuries of being dominated by foreign adversaries, the Chinese people can sense the momentum that comes from rebuilding weakness into strength. Conversely, it can easily be argued the United States is moving in the opposite direction. As a country, we are drowning in division and debt. Worse, our partner is living in an ideological fantasyland that hopes to embrace the very same intellectual nonsense that made China irrelevant in the last century.

Compare what Bernie Sanders and AOC are saying today to what Mao Zedong was saying in 1950—all three of these

Marxist misfits could be grouped together as ideological soul mates.

I don't think Mao could have imagined in his wildest dreams the United States would one day consider its own *Great Leap Forward* into a world where central planners have more power than the sum of their elected citizenry.

This brings us back to the crux of the divorce.

The *dark blue* side of the marriage dreams of a Marxist paradise that has failed in every country it was tried. Their *light blue* cousin is the Democratic Socialist. This latter group envisions a Scandinavian model of peace, tranquility, and high taxes.

In fairness to our Nordic friends, these cultures do consistently score high on the UN quality of life indexes. But perhaps it is easier being happy when others are doing the heavy lifting. Why should the Norwegians worry about owning guns with the US military protecting all of Europe?

Why would countries like Finland and Norway worry about driving away business innovation with high taxes when they have American companies like Google, Apple, Facebook, and Microsoft parading new products out to market each quarter?

And why does a country like Sweden need privatized medicine when pharmaceutical companies like Pfizer, Merck, and Johnson & Johnson are being duly rewarded for their health care innovation by the *US taxpayer*?

Americans have essentially become two very different people, and both sides may be getting closer to a defining revolutionary moment. Democratic socialism can work with small, homogenous populations that value equality over guns and cutthroat competition in the marketplace.

But here's the real marital dilemma: The United States can't become a pacifist country while owning the most advanced nuclear weapons in the world. Just as America won't remain an economic powerhouse if its citizens go the European route of prioritizing thirty-five-hour work weeks over leading the world in innovation.

Something must give in what has become a marriage with irreconcilable differences. I respect most Democrats. I can't imagine a purely libertarian or Republican-led world that would allow corporations to be the primary stewards of society. The United States didn't become the most powerful country by only electing laissez-faire Republican presidents.

America was built not only by the brilliance of Rockefeller, Carnegie, and Ford, but also on the backs of great men and women who belonged to labor unions. I don't want to break apart from millions of good people who bring so much to the marriage. But just as the Republicans dealt with their Joseph McCarthy cancer in 1954, it may be time for the Democrats to either expose their *devil* or risk being consumed by it.

Do not trust Barack Obama to be the Democrat who unmasks the extremists in his party. This would be akin to trusting the fox to guard the henhouse. Barack Obama is a professional agitator with presidential credentials.

I admit, I was surprised to see our ex-president so quiet during Trump's presidency. Obama can be just as loose with the truth as Trump yet come across through the media as introspective, empathetic, and intelligent. Had Trump been a typical GOP president who remained silent, stoic, and guilt ridden—like a Mitt Romney—we would have likely seen much more from Obama on CNN and CNBC.

As we move deeper into a revolutionary environment, expect to see Barack and Michelle Obama make a dramatic return onto the mass-movement stage. Do not expect the Obamas to stop the destruction of monuments, however. Nor will this formidable duo honestly defend previous presidents who are judged to be *on the wrong side of history.*

In Saul Alinsky-fashion, the Obamas will encourage today's protesters to continue their march for *social and economic justice, but* in a *responsible* fashion.

If there is going to be a *marital reconciliation* between Republicans and Democrats, it should never be led by Barack Obama.

Instead pay closer attention to the moderate Democrats in Congress, the media, and in the military. These are the Americans who can be more trusted to expose the cancer that resides in the Democrat Party. And these are the voters who may find the courage to switch sides, particularly if we are willing to compromise in how we build our new political coalition.

In the next chapter, we will discuss how a repurposed Republican Party could have the power to restore democratic normalcy in D.C. In creating a new twenty-first-century platform and party, I am asking the traditionalist to think big and long. Don't misconstrue our upcoming ideas as some attempt at backdoor progressivism. The big-picture goal is to initiate a policy debate that is thought-provoking.

A new platform and party discussion would essentially seek to:

- Avoid the bad divorce option(s) by building a new ruling coalition of White, Black, and Brown voters.
- Replace the establishment GOP platform with a Trump-like doctrine.

Our intent moving forward is not about drawing up precise legislation for Congress. Nor do our tactics have to be limited to a Donald Trump or Joe Biden presidency. Whether political players like Trump, Biden, and Obama remain in the game, or are long gone, our next objective is to either find a way to get along or to consider how both sides can break up.

Chapter 9: A New Republican Party

Those who fail to learn from history are condemned to repeat it.

—*Winston Churchill*

The question the traditionalist must consider today is whether a new political platform could create a mass-movement environment powerful enough to expose the leftist fanatics.

Is it possible to avert a *geographical breakup* by constructing a *New* Republican Party?

If so, how would we go about building such a new platform and movement?

In writing this book, I spoke with a retired US senator who was once a Democrat stalwart in the US Congress. Out of respect for him, I will keep his name anonymous. During our conversation, I asked whether the US was facing a geographical split. This ex-Senator suggested "a future crisis, in conjunction with a unifying president" would be the antidote to our current political dysfunction.

After our conversation, I decided to take a closer look at the mindset of a typical twentieth-century Democrat. I also wanted to better understand how the Democrats and Republicans were able to *work together* and get things done without so much hate and acrimony back then.

So, I went back into history from a hundred years ago with the advantage of hindsight. And believe it or not, 2021 is eerily similar to 1921.

Just like then, America is once again dealing with a global pandemic, a wealth divide, environmental challenges, racial tensions, and a divided Europe. Our primary challenge today, however, isn't about disease, pollution, race, wealth, or Europe.

Our most immediate problem is that the Democrats and Republicans are heading on a collision course toward a fast-track divorce.

If we think about our marital situation in greater detail, today's Republicans are not much different than the GOP from 1921. To the dismay of the progressives, the conservative view of human nature has changed very little over the last hundred years and longer. Just like then, most of today's Republicans reject the notion a handful of elites should have arbitrary power over millions of human beings. Nor do most 2021 conservatives believe human nature is moving closer to equal outcomes and global harmony.

It's really not us who have radically changed the parameters of the marriage; it is our Democrat partner who has veered far beyond the original wedding vows.

How many Democrats from 1921 would have allowed millions of refugees to pour across the southern border with so few questions asked?

How many Democrats from a hundred years ago would have accepted an entire reclassification of gender and marriage without a fight?

And how many 1921 Democrats would have supported academic safe spaces, participation trophies, and the intellectual premise that all White people are privileged?

While the former Senator wouldn't say so, I believe today's twentieth-century Democrats fear the monster they created in turning a blind eye to the radical college professors. Millennial Democrats have bought into the academic narrative that Western society is rigged, corporations are evil, borders should be opened to millions of refugees, and socialism is a virtue.

I don't know if we can put the *Democrat Socialist* genie back into the bottle without an ugly reboot of society. But we owe it to ourselves, and to our great country, to explore every option before we consider the nuclear option of breaking up the country geographically.

The United States is not a third world country with shallow institutions. Is it possible to escape an *ugly divorce* outcome by using hindsight to construct a new political and mass-movement platform that has broader appeal to more Americans? Can we marginalize the cancel culture crazies by overhauling our twentieth-century mission statement?

Fortunately, our problems are not just confined to two people stuck in a bad marriage. In a democracy, the goal doesn't have to be about making *everyone* happy. We just need to move the political needle from 50/50 percent to 55/45 percent. In this sense, I am hopeful the lessons from the last century can help us navigate through the problems of today.

At the university, there was one progressive talking point that was often hard to refute:

Professor:

If there was no progressive movement, there would be no such thing as Social Security. How can any Republican reconcile that Social Security was a bad thing?

When Social Security was enacted in 1935, many twentieth-century Republicans feared the new legislation would bring upon the "death of America." Let's listen to two congressional Republicans from 1935:

> "The lash of the dictator will be felt, and twenty-five million free American citizens will for the first time submit themselves to a fingerprint test." —Rep. Daniel Reed, R-NY[lxxviii]

> "...So vast, so powerful as to threaten the integrity of our institutions and to pull the pillars of the temple down upon the heads of our descendants." —Rep. James W. Wadsworth, R-NY[lxxix]

Unsurprisingly, these conservative congressmen sound a lot like today's anti-government Republicans. To Reed and Wadsworth, a huge governmental takeover spelled the death of democracy and individual liberty. To the progressives, however, the Social Security Act of 1935 promised a future of dignity to those who would otherwise grow old without enough money in the bank.

Eighty years later, who ended up being right? The doom-and-gloom Republicans or the futuristic Democrats?

They were both right.

Yes, *both* sides were right.

But they were also both wrong.

Not everyone can save money, and in 1935, the support structure of an extended family was changing as more rural workers were moving to big cities for factory jobs. Providing an economic safety net to retired Americans was an appropriate consideration for an advanced and changing society.

Who today can imagine a world without a retirement backdrop?

Who can honestly argue that early twentieth-century businesses would have created retirement accounts for their workers without governmental and union pressure?

Unfortunately for us, the two Republican congressmen were also correct in their fears that a big government takeover would lead to further federal encroachment as evidenced by our trillion-dollar debt obligations today.

What good is Social Security if the federal government goes bankrupt? How many trillions of dollars have been wasted since 1935 as the Democrats (and Republicans) learned they could buy votes by creating more federal programs while borrowing against old ones? The right answer in 1935 was probably the creation of a retirement savings program outside of political control.

We're not looking to begin a discussion about privatizing Social Security now. We saw what happened in 2004 when George W. Bush mixed the word "privatization" with Social Security reform. Our point is the twentieth-century progressives were correct in considering a broader safety net for old age.

By staying on the sidelines on the important issue of pension reform, and others like it, the Republicans opened the door to the idea that big government is the answer to every crisis in America.

Our new platform concept is essentially a first mass-movement step that declares our side will no longer be playing by the previous rules of the establishment Republicans (and Democrats). In addition, the plan is about capitalizing on the present weakness of both parties. Uninformed voters are of the perception Republicans only help rich people. Since most people aren't rich, they identify with the Democrats.

Why not create a new movement that aspires to be neutral between employees and employers?

Why not discard an outdated brand that is perceived to be elitist?

If one believes today's Republicans and libertarians don't have any room for improvement, let's look at some statistics. In 1965, the CEO/median pay ratio between the boss and his/her workers was about 20:1.[lxxx]

Today, that number is closer to 300:1.[lxxxi] In the global economy, fewer than one hundred people have more wealth than the bottom three billion.[lxxxii]

CEOs seem to have few moral dilemmas in personally making billions of dollars with one hand and paying out twelve dollars per hour with the other hand. Many bosses have little quandary spending a holiday weekend in the Caribbean while their employees are working a Black Friday away from their families.

Established business models that were profitable for decades can become obsolete in months, not years. Yes, the economists can argue innovation increases productivity, and that everything will work out in the end. But the long run is not always nice to a forty-five-year-old worker who spent a lifetime mastering only one or two skill sets.

Today, sixty percent of Americans are on a path of having *zero* savings when they retire.[lxxxiii] If you are rich and think you're safe, you may want to think again. In a democracy, one doesn't want to be on the ten percent team. The college professors are already training a new band of radicals in how to pursue after-tax money from older Americans with above-average bank accounts.

What is wrong in considering private-sector improvements to 401(k) pension plans? What value is there to a 401(k) if an employee doesn't have the extra funds to build a retirement nest egg? How is it that some profitable companies offer 1:1 matches to their employees, while others who are equally profitable offer nothing?

Why are so many wealthy Americans oblivious to the Marxist alligators lurking just outside their doors? Do the *progressive one-percenters* really think they will find atonement by voting for Democrats? And at what point does one have enough money in life? More importantly, how much wealth does a person need before they begin to see the bigger picture?

I am suggesting we consider getting ahead of today's cancel culture radicals—not only with pension reform but also with wages and health care. If a new political movement can establish a better compact between employees and employers in the workplace, is there a chance we could marginalize today's Marxist academics? More importantly, isn't incentivizing employers to share profits during successful years good public policy?

Our new platform plan isn't about squeezing small-business start-ups with the expectation of profit sharing. Nor should companies be expected to be financially burdened during poor or average years. Our goal, rather, is to think about using different economic and political vehicles that are flexible and more balanced toward finding a greater employee/employer equilibrium.

Let's begin with some low-hanging fruit. Nowadays, someone who makes a million dollars annually by running a small business pays 37 percent in federal income taxes.[lxxxiv] Conversely, someone who makes a million dollars flipping high-end real estate only pays 20 percent in capital gains taxes.[lxxxv] This goes back to Warren Buffet's argument that his secretary pays more in taxes than he does.

Why not consider an economic platform that says anyone who makes a million dollars must pay the 37 percent tax regardless of how the money was earned? Yes, the establishment

Republicans will crow about a previous alternative minimum tax that was wrought with unintended consequences. But how can it be that difficult to implement a uniform level of taxation regardless of how the million dollars was made?

The "death tax" is another issue the Republicans have spun to their political advantage. Most of us don't understand the inheritance tax only applies to an individual with over *11.58 million dollars* in assets.[lxxxvi] Yet, in future election cycles, we can almost predict with certainty the GOP will try to eliminate the *death tax* because the term conjures up images of the federal government trying to confiscate the hundred thousand dollars average-Joe planned on leaving to his kids when he passes away.

Instead of playing games with the public, give the very wealthy two choices upon death: Either pay taxes on any wealth accumulated beyond a certain threshold or give the money to a charity of their choice. Why would any society want to see a billionaire's kids inherit five billion dollars? And what billionaire would be stupid enough to hand their hard-earned money over to the federal government in lieu of a private charity?

In what could best be described as an Andrew Carnegie approach to advancing society, the choice of giving billions of dollars to a charity versus giving the money to the government would incentivize the wealthiest citizens to put their talents to work for all of society. Even liberal billionaires are smart enough to understand giving money to the government is like throwing wealth into a black hole. And policies such as eliminating tax loopholes and forcing billionaires to give back to society are political winners with most voters.

Now, let's move the needle a little further. Should company owners be required to post their CEO/median employee pay ratio? This type of legislation is already in place for some public companies,[lxxxvii] but the guidelines are easy to manipulate due to the myriad of loopholes that can be used to disguise CEO compensation. In addition, today's laws don't require privately held companies to display this data. Why not support a political platform that requires *all* businesses to show such information? This mechanism would allow employees the right to go online to compare their boss's pay ratio to other owners in the same field.

Again, hear me out. When my business began to gain traction, I had a great team of people who believed in me. As the company grew, I always promised *the team* we would find the "Promised Land" of making big money and being the best at what we did. After years of growing pains, that big day finally arrived. At the time, my company had thirty employees, a million dollars in leftover profits, and no debt.

What was the *right* thing to do with the money?

Sure, I was the founder and sole individual responsible for litigation, problems, and payrolls, but what about the team? Without them, the million dollars wouldn't be sitting in the bank.

I ended up keeping half and giving the other half away as year-end bonuses. This may not sound like the stuff of Robin Hood, but keep in mind I assumed ownership of a company with three hundred thousand dollars of debt. For years, our competitors predicted employees would become bitter once the bonuses came to an end. But the doomsayers were wrong. Even in the down years of 2009-10, our entire company took pay cuts with no bonuses. There were few defections or morale problems during the Great Recession, and over time, our company attracted the best talent in the industry. We became a juggernaut in our respective field, and that first million-dollar profit-sharing program multiplied as the company grew larger.

By the end of my career, the CPA was returning millions of dollars back to a great team of people nearly every year. And our business wasn't some kind of Fortune 500 company. Yet, each successful year, we had to warn the local banks to carry millions of dollars in cash on hand for the second Friday of each December.

I'm not looking for a pat on the back here. As a leader who built a committed team, I simply couldn't rationalize the idea of keeping all the profits for myself. And in taking this approach, other ripples began to occur throughout an entire industry.

Before our company began the trend of large, year-end bonuses, the industry norm around Christmas was to hand out Walmart gift certificates. Once word got out about the bonuses, however, the Walmart debit cards took a backseat to nice end-of-year profit-sharing checks at many of my competitors.

No, my gratuitousness wasn't always appreciated by other company owners. But as I reflect in time, sharing big profit years in such an unusual fashion was the most rewarding business decision I ever made, bar none.

There should be more to being a CEO than simply keeping shareholders happy. Barack Obama already started things when he told business owners, "You didn't build that..."[lxxxviii]

The libertarian CEO who hates intrusion in the marketplace is likely to be the same person whose Yale-educated children revere Bernie Sanders. If the traditionalist doesn't figure out a way to make pay, health care expenses, and pensions more equitable, the next wave of lefties will have no problem piercing IRAs, bank accounts, and safe-deposit boxes. Our twenty-first-century business leaders can be proactive, or they can face the ugly alternative at their own peril.

I often think about the idea of a new, twenty-first-century labor union model. There should be little debate that unions helped build the middle class of the last century. Unfortunately, many unions have lost their way in today's global economy. As a construction contractor who worked in the unionized factories, I saw the best and worst unions have to offer. While some unions have modernized themselves to be relevant in a fast-moving economy, most remain prehistoric relics stuck in a twentieth-century mindset. To this day, I am shocked many of the steel and auto plants in the Rustbelt States are still in business.

If today's unions are not up to the task of being relevant in a twenty-first-century economy, why not go around them with official public policy?

For example, why not mandate by federal law that retail workers should be paid double time wages on Sundays and holidays at larger companies?

Why not consider legislation that triggers higher employee 401(k) contributions once the boss breaks a 50:1 CEO/median pay threshold?

I understand some industries with less-skilled workers and lower wages could skew the median pay formula and vice versa. But can anyone honestly say a company like Amazon shouldn't be forced to contribute a larger 401(k) match when Jeff Bezos pays himself *1.2 million* times the $28,000 median pay of his workforce?[lxxxix]

I have also been thinking about Elizabeth Warren's "wealth tax." Her 2020 campaign plan was to fund Medicare-for-all by levying a tax on accumulated wealth beyond fifty million dollars.[xc] The tax would have to be paid every year—it would not have been a one-time deal.[xci] Warren's proposal would have resulted in an incredible wealth transfer of over 300 billion dollars *every year* forward![xcii]

We'll get back to health care in a moment, but what about the idea of taxing billionaires a *one-time,* after-tax hit that wipes out the student debt bubble? I acknowledge this type of talk sounds like it is coming from a Bernie Sanders campaign rally. But the students didn't create the college debt problem—the adults did. The government should have never involved themselves in student loans in the first place. The result of the politicians moving into the loan business was a big economic bubble and a diluted piece of paper.

With our "billionaire plan," those who honored their student debt loans would be paid retroactively in the same proportion as the students who haven't paid back their loans. In addition, the larger universities would take part in the bailout plan with an endowment tax. The universities went right along with the nonsense that "everybody should go to college." They borrowed heavily to fund expansions, and they devalued the prestige of a college degree by accepting too many unqualified students and professors.

Can anyone honestly say a four-year soft degree is worth more than a high school diploma from thirty years ago?

How many of today's college graduates are capable of drafting a workplace email that meets only the most basic level of professional scrutiny?

I acknowledge the slippery slope that comes with buying into Elizabeth Warren's billionaire tax logic. Once this door opens, it may never shut. But we may want to consider the future gamble of helping millennials at the expense of billionaires and universities. If society can raise the former out of debt, there is some hope they will eventually find the sense to rejoin their parents and grandparents in the bigger fight of getting our democracy healthy again.

Now, let's expand our political-platform conversation beyond pensions, wages, and the student debt crisis. Let's begin with the contentious issue of health care.

Health Care

The US spends more in health care than any other country.[xciii] As such, much of the world's innovation in medicine comes from the American free market system. In many respects, the US consumer is subsidizing a disproportionate share of the research and development costs for every other country in the world.

In this coronavirus era, what other country could have produced *multiple* vaccinations in less than twelve months?

How many medical blockbusters are coming out of the nationally managed health care systems of Canada and Norway?

With a government-run system, money gets lost in the bureaucracy, and there is little incentive to invent billion-dollar medical treatments. With a market system, big corporate profits are made because the individual consumer has no incentive to shop prices. If a typical person has a shoulder injury, he or she doesn't care if the doctor charges five thousand dollars or twenty-five thousand dollars—the patient is primarily interested in timing and convenience. We all know friends who won't visit a doctor unless they are close to death. And we all probably know someone who will go to an emergency room for a pregnancy test.

The final answer in our never-ending health care debate probably lies in a better-defined public/private partnership. Government would have a role in mandating that older and sicker patients don't fall through the cracks of a privately run system. Health care providers could be mandated to be more transparent with their pricing. And both the government and the private sector should incentivize healthy lifestyles, health savings accounts, and price shopping with nonemergency medical situations.

In addition, the US should prevent other countries from cherry-picking its innovation and charging lower prices to its individual citizens.

Why are we paying more for American-made pharmaceuticals than Canadians and Europeans? Should it not be mandated by law that US citizens can't be charged more for *homegrown* prescription drugs than people in other developed nations?

Why is the United States allowing so many "socialist" democracies to freeload off its privatized system?

Just like 1921, the traditionalist can be proactive on issues like health care, or he/she can let the other side eventually dictate the terms of the debate. If we continue to stall the very complex issue of health care, one thing is nearly certain: the US will end up with a Medicare-for-all solution. And the West could find itself in the unenviable position of relying on China for future health care innovation.

The Environment

In the twentieth century, there were dust bowls exasperated by shortsighted land use policies.[xciv] Today, the primary environmental issue of our era is the threat of climate change. I don't know how much truth there is to climate change being radically impacted by human beings. It's difficult trusting meteorologists who predict weather patterns a week from now, let alone twenty years from now.

While in college, I also witnessed how the left senses a tremendous opportunity in linking capitalism to the horrific images of a hotter planet. Future planetary catastrophe and apocalypse induced by greedy millionaires and billionaires solves the spiritual dilemma of a Marxist ideology that lacks a devil, heaven, and hell.

Ignoring the environment because we hate the Marxists and the tree huggers, though, is not the proper way forward. There is visible evidence to support the premise the environment has big problems.

Flotillas of plastic and garbage bigger than the state of Texas are floating in the oceans.[xcv]

And one doesn't have to be a scientist to understand the carbon buildup associated with several billion additional human beings driving gas-powered vehicles.

Why not adopt a new environmental platform that says consumer plastics must be discontinued within the next five years? Why not be the first country to realize a 90 percent alternative automobile market?

Our new platform can be both pro-capitalism and pro-environment. We don't have to play the silly game of picking one at the expense of the other. And we *don't* have to be so easily typecast as the political party of polluters and deniers of science.

Race in America

Today, I can't reference my "Black friends" because this type of "talk" is loaded with racist overtones. This being said, I can't imagine a breakup that leaves behind those Black and biracial Americans who love the United States and simply want to move beyond the politics of skin color.

Contrary to what the media says, *both* Democrats and Republicans want to see Black Americans prosper. The question is how do we get there as a society.

Are double standards and trillions of additional dollars in debt the answer in uniting Whites and Blacks?

Or are stable families and good schools the best way in offering equal opportunity to all?

The present-day dynamic of *White empathy* combined with *Black wokeness* could be the spark that moves the United States into an *ugly divorce.* I'm under no illusion of what the racial stakes are in this context of time.

But let us clarify again—any future mass movement that prioritizes skin color over individual character will ultimately fail.

Should there be a successful realignment in US politics, the "New America" will be Black, Brown, and White.

To those Blacks who are willing to bid goodbye to yesterday, I say, "Come on in, and join the new movement. Be bold, and join traditional Whites in culture, friendship, and matrimony." But to those Blacks, Browns, and Whites who want to remain in the past, fighting the same fights over-and-over again, I offer this future advice—be ready to sleep in the same bed together.

Twenty-First-Century Morality

In this era of secular indifference, should a repurposed United States consider codifying a *twenty-first-century Ten Commandments*?

How long can any civilization remain viable when its ten-year-old children have instant access to hard-core pornography on their cell phones?

To this day, no psychologist has discovered a road map for human affairs that is more profound than what the ancients assembled thousands of years ago. Whether one believes in the literal interpretations of the holy books or not, the intellect and foresight of those great minds was incredible. Yet today, we continue to run away from our founding principles to pursue a secularist existence where *equality* is prioritized above every other moral consideration.

Should Karl Marx have more societal standing than Moses, Jesus, Plato, and Locke? Is there any content in the UN Human Rights Manual that has equal footing to the Aristotelian notion that individual balance and virtue are the antidotes to excess and arrogance?

The United States was founded on Judeo-Christian values, the writings of the ancient Greeks, and enlightened European thinkers. If some people are offended by these original covenants, they can easily pick another civilization. As such, a new platform should clarify Judeo-Christian covenants like the Golden Rule and the Ten Commandments are once again welcomed in every public building.

In terms of the gender debate, I acknowledge most of Generations Y and Z have bought into the logic of gender being *fluid*. And I acknowledge the constitutional difficulties associated with reversing the 2015 Supreme Court decision on marriage (*Obergefell v. Hodges*). But as society blows past the previous two percent benchmark of people being *born* gay, opinions on the origin of gender can hopefully be questioned with science and not just with progressive ideology.[xcvi]

The issue of gender and marriage is simply too important to not be included in a mass-movement platform. Is there anything more vital to the continuation of human society than biologically vested men and women bringing new life into the world as one? And how long do we want to keep giving young children *dozens of gender choices*?

Moving beyond race, gender, and morality, the hope is a bold new manifesto could have the power to break today's red-and-blue stalemate. The goal with this strategy would be to awaken, energize, and unify everyday Americans to fight back against the elites in academia, government, and big tech.

In essence, we would replace the twentieth-century Republican doctrine with a Trump-like platform that is pro-America, pro-worker, pro-business, and *anti-swamp*.

We would radically overhaul education from top to bottom.

We would argue why society should be centered around two genders and strong family structures.

And we would seek to unify Blacks, Browns, and Whites beyond the divisive allure of identity politics.

I admit our "new Republican Party" idea may not be a strong enough medicine for such a deeply divided country. But is there a chance a traditionalist-led mass movement could secure the middle-class center while pinning the far-left radicals into a permanent state of irrelevance?

Moreover, could a successful realignment in US politics finally pin the bullseye directly on the source that created our problems in the first place—the intellectuals in academia and their pawns in Washington D.C?

Our goal with the new platform/party concept is not about trying to fool millions of people with a bait-and-switch. It is about rediscovering ourselves to meet great challenges while acknowledging we are inextricably linked to the traditions of the past. Let's step outside our Republican and libertarian playbooks and ask each other some important questions:

- Should a new political platform codify certain elements of Judeo-Christian teachings into official public policy?
- Is today's compact between private workers and multinational corporations too one-sided?
- Should an unexpected health care event have the power to ruin a life savings?
- Is doing nothing about the environment an option in a global reality where plastic bottles are ending up in the stomachs of whales and dolphins?

If the traditionalist stays timid and inflexible, he/she will lose in the same fashion the Republicans did a hundred years ago. But instead of losing out to an FDR, the Republicans could lose to a future anti-American globalist.

Why not get ahead of today's dysfunction by thinking big, expanding the tent, and suffocating the true *cancer* in the marriage?

We will know our *good divorce* plan is taking root should a solid majority of voters move beyond the fault lines that define today's dysfunctional marriage. In addition, we will know our new political movement concept is gaining traction should some of the following conditions begin to occur:

- The GOP, as we know it today, is completely overhauled.

- The leadership of the new "traditionalist" party becomes less White and less male.
- More Blacks begin to publicly denounce progressive politicians and policies.
- The Democratic Party disassociates itself with its cancel culture extremists.
- More liberal intellectuals and celebrities break ranks in a public fashion.
- Brown Americans move politically closer to traditional Whites.
- More women associate words like "empathy" and "social justice" with ineffective big government and insincere politicians.
- More Americans demand a radical overhaul of K-12 education.
- Public and private universities see a noticeable decline in stature, including bankruptcies, closures, and diminished tenure protection.

What happens if our new political platform/party idea never occurs? What are our options if today's tensions escalate? We will know our marriage is taking a turn for the worse should some of these circumstances play out:

- A Trump loss elevates the divorce fault lines.
- Traditional red states turn blue, creating a potential permanent imbalance of national political power.
- Individual states blatantly disregard the federal government and the US Constitution.
- An unexpected crisis results in widespread civil unrest.
- A federal debt crisis occurs with real-life consequences.
- A persistent escalation of racial protests and violence takes root in more American cities.

- States, counties, and cities attempt to unilaterally secede from the US.
- Browns move politically and culturally closer to Blacks and Marxist Whites.
- The US military breaks its code of silence on politics.

If America takes a turn for the bad, what is our Plan B? Most of us are not looking to see the US split geographically, but as with most potential divorces, we owe it to ourselves to discuss the best- and worst-case outcomes in an attorney's office.

If our future destiny is headed down a path of ugliness, we need to better understand what that ugliness could look like.

It is now time to analyze the real-world ramifications associated with a geographical breakup of the United States of America.

Chapter 10: The Revolutionary Gamble of the Century

If you look at the map of the United States, there is all that red in the middle, places where Trump won. What the map doesn't show you is that I won the places that own two-thirds of America's gross domestic product. I won the places that are optimistic, diverse, dynamic, moving forward.

—Hillary Clinton

There exists the chance the US is already beyond the point of simple repair. America may once again be facing an 1860's set of revolutionary circumstances. We know how much life and treasure was lost in the *first* Civil War. What lessons can we learn from the past as we contemplate a *second* geographical breakup?

Today, both sides can make an argument for going it alone. At first glance, it seems like the "blue" states are in a stronger position to secede from the "red" states.[xcvii] Since the Great Recession, red and blue states have been traveling down divergent paths when it comes to income, education, and GDP growth.[xcviii] At our universities, blue states are typecast as hip, diverse, and cool, whereas red states are looked down upon as old, White, rural, and angry.

In progressive circles, there is much talk about which US states are *net givers* and which are *net takers*. That is, the difference between what an individual state pays into the federal government in taxes versus what it receives back from the feds in services.

Using data from the Rockefeller Institute of Government, blue states like New York appear to be heavily subsidizing red states like Mississippi.[xcix] For every dollar New York pays into the federal government, they are only getting back eighty-six cents.[c] Conversely, for every dollar Mississippi pays, they are getting back double.[ci]

Is it possible the so-called fiscally conservative red states would go broke first if the US were to splinter off into two countries?

As we contemplate the far-reaching concept of breaking up the US by geography, let's begin by addressing the flawed logic of people like Hillary Clinton and the NYT's Paul Krugman. These liberal talking heads are attempting to paint the picture that blue America is moving forward, while red is assumingly going backwards.

If we take a closer look at the Rockefeller data, however, states that are home to America's military bases stand out when federal outflows are weighted against what the IRS brings in revenues.[cii] Military bases equate to a greater share of federal dollars. This reality explains why blue states with large military presences like Virginia, Maryland, and New Mexico score just as poorly on the Rockefeller rankings as red states like Kentucky and Louisiana.[ciii]

Secondly, states with higher levels of means-tested entitlements also skew the inflow/outflow data. Yes, it is true red states like Arkansas are drawing in significant federal dollars compared to other states.[civ] And yes, the statistics show New York and California appear to be getting a raw deal—especially with Trump's tax plan.[cv] What is the inconvenient little secret in the *backwoods* red states?

A third of the population in states like Mississippi, Louisiana, and Arkansas are Black—a specific demographic that statistically takes in more dollars than it pays out in federal taxes.[cvi] What would the inflow/outflow ratios of lily-white blue states like Vermont and Connecticut look like if these demographics were reversed?[cvii]

In fact, *why isn't there more diversity in Bernie Sanders' home state of Vermont?*

Lastly, life is also more complicated than just creating GDP. Take a guess at what states have the *fewest* military veterans per capita.

- Illinois
- Massachusetts
- California
- New Jersey
- New York

And which states have the *most* military veterans per capita?

- Alaska
- Montana
- Virginia
- Maine
- Oklahoma[cviii]

The *unenlightened* red-state citizens are more likely to fight and die for their country than their blue-state counterparts. And it is the red-state "deplorables" who are most likely to farm, build, and produce energy for both the blue and red states.[cix]

We can all agree Silicon Valley is important to the success of America. But so are the Permian Basin and Great Plains regions of the country.

Also, what is to say the *blue states* would keep their GDP advantage should *any divorce* go public?

When the Civil War began, seven slave-holding states— South Carolina, Mississippi, Florida, Alabama, Georgia, Louisiana, and Texas—were the first to secede from the Union.[cx] They were later joined by North Carolina, Virginia, Arkansas, and Tennessee.[cxi] The issue of slavery was succinct, and big money was involved. Before the Civil War, the South was powerful because cotton was the biggest driver of the US economy.[cxii]

Of interest to us, the *GDP creators* in both regions *didn't* defect to the other side. They stayed put in their own backyards.

This distinction brings us back to another important history lesson. What makes liberals like Clinton and Krugman so confident companies based in blue states today wouldn't pack up and move to a newly formed "Red America" should a second breakup occur?

What is to say today's woke companies wouldn't bail if an AOC became their future blue-state president?

The 1860's North and South were also unified in their respective causes. Today, there is no such unity in the Democrat Party. Half of the progressives are anti-capitalists. What makes the leftist elites so confident highly taxed venues like Manhattan and Silicon Valley aren't capable of becoming economic ghost towns tomorrow?

Abraham Lincoln is an icon revered for protecting the Union at nearly any cost. In what is an uncommon critique of Lincoln's decision to use war to prevent secession, Robert F. Hawes Jr., author of *One Nation Indivisible?: A Study of Secession and the Constitution,* argues that Lincoln would have been better off allowing the Southern states to go their own way without a fight.[cxiii] Hawes claims that by using the full force of the federal government, and even violating the US Constitution, Lincoln not only lost unnecessary life and treasure, but also the original intent of federalism and limited government.

Yes, Abraham Lincoln is nearly untouchable in his degree of wisdom, courage, and statesmanship, but was he wrong in not allowing the South to simply secede unencumbered?

Should Abraham Lincoln have let the South simply wither away over time instead of initiating such a violent show of federal power?

Using Hawes's logic, there was a reasonable chance the 1860s South could have seceded in 1861, the North could have said farewell, and both sides could have pursued their own experiments without war. There is also a chance the South could have rejoined the Union after realizing it was wrong on the issue of slavery. Had this second course of action played out, America could have theoretically avoided its most costly war. In addition, the South could have handled the aftermath of slavery without big-brother-North pointing a gun to its head.[cxiv]

Why does this matter to us today?

As Americans, we have been taught to believe the states are inseparable. Maybe this line of thinking was appropriate in 1861 when the US was more vulnerable to foreign adversaries, and maybe this logic still has merit today. But it is also possible the fifty states no longer need each other in the same way they did in the nineteenth century. It is thus feasible a twenty-first-century United States could break off into two countries without the pretext of a bloody war.

Today, we hear about states like California and Texas seceding from the Union. Is it possible an individual state, or a group of states, could send a letter to the president and the Senate saying, "Let this correspondence serve as notice that California no longer considers itself a member state in the US. It is hereby our intention to negotiate a release from the US, its laws, and its Constitution."?

The US Constitution is silent on the idea of a state, or a group of states, seceding from the Union. Article IV, Section 3, Clause 1, only outlines the issue of adding additional states to the Union:

> New States may be admitted by the Congress into this Union; but no new State shall be formed or erected within the Jurisdiction of any other State; nor any State be formed by the junction of two or more States, or Parts of States, without the Consent of the Legislatures of the States concerned as well as Congress.[cxv]

Some states' rights advocates have argued that since state sovereignty predates the US Constitution, individual states have a natural right to leave any federal government deemed unjust. This talking point goes back to the founding and was carried into the Civil War. In 1869, however, the Supreme Court ruled in *Texas v. White* that "unilateral secession is unconstitutional," while commenting that only *"revolution or consent of the states could lead to a successful secession."*[cxvi]

More recently, the late conservative Supreme Court Justice Antonin Scalia said, "If there was any constitutional issue resolved by the Civil War, it is that no state has the right to secede."[cxvii]

Let's be clear about unilateral secession occurring in America. Barring an explosive set of revolutionary circumstances, this type of approach is not going to be the vehicle used to divide the US into two countries.

The Supreme Court would never allow state(s) to secede unless the measure was constitutionally approved; that is, ratification by two-thirds majorities in the House and Senate, and thirty-eight state legislatures. Moreover, why would any blue state vote in favor of losing California's fifty-five electoral votes? The same goes for Texas and the other red states. In this sense, secession talk in California, Texas, and others is only conjecture.

In today's delicate balance of power, both blue and red states need every player on the team. If there is going to be a geographical divide, the plan is more likely to be hatched in the setting of a constitutional convention.

Under Article V, the founders scripted two ways to convene a convention. The first method is initiated in Congress by a two-thirds vote in both houses and then ratified by three-fourths of the state's legislatures. Of the twenty-seven amendments made to the Constitution, this amendment process has been used exclusively.

The second method in amending the Constitution was intended to give states constitutional authority without consent from the federal government. Under this latter Article V provision, a convention can be held when two-thirds of state legislatures call to order a constitutional meeting.[cxviii] Listed below is the verbiage that allows both methods:

Article V, US Constitution

"The Congress, whenever two thirds of both houses shall deem it necessary, shall propose amendments to this Constitution, or, on the application of the legislatures of two thirds of the several states, shall call a convention for proposing amendments, which, in either case, shall be valid to all intents and purposes, as part of this Constitution, when ratified by the legislatures of three fourths of the several states, or by conventions in three fourths thereof, as the one or the other mode of ratification may be proposed by the Congress; provided that no amendment which may be made prior to the year one thousand eight hundred and eight shall in any manner affect the first and fourth clauses in the ninth section of the first article; and that no state, without its consent, shall be deprived of its equal suffrage in the Senate."[cxix]

Is our way out of a bad marriage an invocation of an Article V convention?

Some legal scholars have argued that an open-ended convention could blow up the entire Constitution. Let's again listen to Justice Scalia in 2014: "I certainly would not want a constitutional convention. Whoa! Who knows what would come out of it?"[cxx] It is certainly understandable a constitutional originalist like Scalia would have feared such an event could turn the entire document upside down. But much has changed since Justice Scalia died in 2016.

The US could be on the brink of a revolution. Trying to safeguard the Constitution when the walls of the house are collapsing is akin to grabbing onto a tree during a tornado. If we can't stop the barbarians from destroying national monuments, how long will it be before the anarchists start breaking down the windows of the National Archives Building?[cxxi]

Using the state-sponsored mechanism in Article V, it would take thirty-four states to convene a convention with participation from all fifty states. In this era of hyper-partisanship, it is reasonable to assume thirty-four state legislatures would authorize such a gathering. Let's not forget that blue states despise us as much as we dislike them.

Whether a constitutional convention is convened by the states or Congress, the goal would be about getting both sides together to either *save the marriage or to discuss moving on with the least amount of pain.*

Yes, this Article V talk carries significant risks. In an era where race relations are deteriorating and monuments are being knocked down, a convention would almost certainly expose old wounds. But short of an unexpected reconciliation between red/blue, Black/White, and Black/Brown/White what other choices do we have as a country?

There is a chance both sides could *geographically divorce* and be much happier than they are today. Should there be a split in the US, it doesn't have to be violent. Look at our relationship with Canada. Canadians may be more progressive than Californians, yet despite our differences, they are a good neighbor and a great trading partner.

Yes, Canada is fortunate to live next door to a neighbor who has the guns and fortitude to keep bad actors out of North America. But they are also a trusted ally.

A second divorce doesn't have to evolve into an ugly civil war. Both sides could structure a gradual breakup while maintaining mutual trade and commerce. Maybe one side will fail and be at the mercy of their former partner. Or maybe both sides will succeed and finally find the freedom to be who they want to be. Most importantly, *all of us* will be able to vote with our feet once the terms of the divorce are finalized.

Since the Article V verbiage is so vague, every source of tension would be fair game at a convention. There would be no filibusters, clotures, or gavels in such a setting. By today's standards, an invocation of an Article V Convention could be viewed as a no-holds-barred discussion where everything is on the table:

- How does America overcome the original sin of slavery?
- What are the pros and cons in dividing the United States of America?
- What would the national security ramifications associated with *two Americas* be?
- How would the national debt be accounted for?
- Would any re-created borders be "hard" or "soft"?

Under such an incredible set of circumstances, the thought police would be placed on official notice. When lives, families, and careers are at stake, there will be little time for politically correct conversations.

It would, in fact, be fascinating to watch an open convention play out on primetime television. Millions of Americans would be glued to their TVs, listening as both sides passionately debate the cultural, political, and philosophical issues of our era. An unfiltered convention would have the potential to drive voter passions to levels not witnessed since the Civil War.

Where do the liberals and traditionalists stand on Jefferson's Declaration of Independence? Would either side want to change this iconic document? If so, how?

And what about the US Constitution—would either side dare alter the most transformative piece of paper in human history?

A constitutional convention would allow blue- and red-state representatives to present their twenty-first-century manifestos to the public. This type of event would carry real-world ramifications to every US citizen. Politicians on both sides would speak extensively in back rooms about future alliances, redrawn borders, strategic advantages/disadvantages, federalism, and money. It is even possible Canada and Mexico could join the discussion(s.)

Should a convention lead to the discussion of breaking up the country, the list of negotiating points would be initially endless.

Both sides would seek to reshape "two new Americas" to align with their views of philosophy, morality, and politics. While *red* Americans would likely prioritize limited government, constitutional originalism, and Judeo-Christian values, what would *blue* Americans prioritize?

In the spirit of universalism, would a newly created Blue America accept every global applicant for immediate citizenship? If Red America were to tighten the requirements associated with voting and citizenship, would the new Blue America accept all transfer-requests with no strings attached?

Further, if one is a red-state American living in a newly formed Blue America, what would their options be? Could they still live in a blue state and pay taxes into a newly formed Red America? If a blue-state voter ended up residing in a red state, would their right to vote apply to Red America, Blue America, or both? Yes, there would be certain societal covenants that newly created Blue and Red Americas may agree on. Both would likely maintain their obligations of paying into Social Security and Medicare. But what about currency?

During the Civil War, the Confederacy printed the "Greyback," but the paper money was never backed by anything more than a promise of victory over the North.[cxxii] After the war was over, the Confederate currency was worthless. How would both sides resolve the issue of money today? And beyond the significant question of debt and currency, there are other complex negotiating dilemmas like national defense, citizenship rights, property rights, and treaty obligations.

Is it possible the revolutionary sparks flying from a courtroom-like battle could have the potential to wake up those apathetic Americans sitting on the sidelines?

First- and second-generation Brown Americans, for example, would come to understand there is more to American-style liberty than taking easy multiple-choice exams to gain citizenship. Would Latinos and Asians choose open borders, free stuff, and high taxes, or would they pick an America that values traditional definitions of gender, an entrepreneurial business environment, and limited government?

Would Black Americans be suspicious of the do-gooder Whites and their big bag of freebies? Could a geographical split have the power of doing what Lincoln couldn't do 150 years ago—unite Whites and Blacks with shared values instead of forced assimilation? Or would most Blacks leave the newly formed Red America fearing personal accountability, strong families, and a merit-based society are backdoor ways of legalizing *systematic racism*?

What about Generations Y and Z?

A constitutional convention would be a lot more exciting for younger Americans than listening to boring history professors. Would younger Americans pick open genders and free stuff over the traditional triage of God, family, and country? Maybe. But either way, they would live to witness one of the biggest social science experiments in the history of mankind. In the end, the millennials may finally discover the answers to today's great divide:

- Can human nature be molded to one day guarantee global harmony and equal outcomes?
- Which political ideology leads to greater satisfaction and purpose in life—nanny-state governance policed by central planners or individual liberty protected by guns?
- Are traditional parents and grandparents unenlightened stooges for the bourgeoisie, or are older Whites the last line of defense against tyranny and authoritarian rule?

Geographically, over ninety percent of the country votes Republican.[cxxiii] Democrats monopolize coastal regions, university towns, and urban areas. If a constitutional convention led to the radical notion of breaking up the country by region, states as we know them today would likely be redrawn with name changes. It is easy to say, "Give the Democrats the East and West Coasts, and we'll take the rest."

But should such a split occur, states like California and New York would likely splinter inside and outside their present-day borders. If one were to drive forty minutes beyond downtown LA and New York City, there are millions of Americans who wouldn't want anything to do with their big-city cousins once any divorce went public.

Should an Article V Convention result in a land split, a newly rejuvenated Red America could repurpose Republican apathy and dysfunction into a future foundation of hope, optimism, and purpose. This type of *redo* would allow the traditionalist to put their *new United States* on solid footing for future generations.

Young and old would become united by the kinship that comes with going into battle as one.

Like-minded Blacks and Whites would say goodbye to Uncle Tom and the ghosts of slavery.

Latinos and Asians would no longer be walking in the limbo land of divided Whites. And the days of using labels like African American, Hispanic American, and Muslim American would officially end. Instead of feeling guilty and divided, a new Red America would be uplifted by big ideas and freed from the tyranny of political correctness.

As for our ex-partners, maybe they can finally find their real-world utopia without having us standing in their way.

In what could become the ultimate game of revolutionary poker, blue could finally move beyond America's history of racism, privilege, and inequality and make everything right with the various victim classes. Without Republican obstruction, a new Blue America could easily implement free college, abolish the use of fossil fuels, grant reparations to Blacks, and open their borders to every global refugee.

Is it possible that having a more public and radical discussion in a raucous convention environment could flush out the leftist radicals in the same way McCarthy was exposed in the 1950s?

Maybe. But it is more likely that once the door of an Article V Convention is opened, there will be no turning back. In the end, an open convention could be judged in the context of history as the first formalized step of a *third* American divorce.[2]

There are, of course, no guarantees an open Article V Convention would happen in today's cutthroat era of politics— just as there is a chance an actual convention could make things even worse than they already are today.

What happens if our convention idea blows up into a frenzy and nothing gets resolved? What is the backup plan should an Article V Convention never occur? The next step in our process is to take a walk down the hypothetical road of our first ugly divorce.

Donald Trump's election victory in 2016 may not have been a democratic accident. Trump would have never been elected to the presidency if we were living in stable times.

Trump, whether intended or not, has forever changed the rules of engagement. Politically, President Trump was the belligerent uncle who crashed the passive-aggressive family party where tension was always lingering behind the small talk

---

[2] For reference, the author suggests the Revolutionary War was Divorce #1, and the US Civil War was Divorce #2.

and fake smiles. He sowed chaos and initiated unpleasant conversations in every corner of the room.

And like the family of the crazy uncle, things will never be the same in US politics.

What happens to our mass-movement plan if Trump is gone? Obviously, the other side would be incredibly happy. But what would *we* do?

Conversely, what are the mass-movement possibilities if Trump decides to make a *comeback*? Should we give an ex-president a revolutionary handbook that dares to break up the union of the United States of America?

Chapter 11: An Ugly American Divorce

Pick the target, freeze it, personalize it, and polarize it. Cut off the support network and isolate the target from sympathy.

—*Saul Alinsky*

Whereas many Republicans find horror in a progressive presidency, there exists the possibility a Trump exit could result in a civil reboot opportunity. The mass-movement problem with Donald Trump is that half of the country despises him. Throughout his four years as president, Trump was bailing water out of the *Titanic* with a five-gallon bucket.

While an insider president could incite the conditions required for a future societal reboot, he would ultimately be held responsible for any civil disobedience that occurred under his watch. In the context of a revolutionary environment, Trump could simply be more impactful from the outside than from the inside.

We are once again moving into the world of *ugly* and *unpredictable*. As we consider *changing the rules of the game*, let's begin the process by formally introducing two twentieth-century historians who wrote extensively about mass-movement and revolutionary theory.

The late historian Crane Brinton analyzed the conditions associated with the British, American, French, and Russian Revolutions. Brinton believed revolutionary conditions arise from inept governance and unfair taxation; a transfer of allegiance from the intellectual classes; and division between the old ruling classes of society.[cxxiv] Brinton hypothesized revolutions "must be made respectable and must touch the soul."[cxxv]

Importantly, he observed that all four revolutions shared prior upward growth followed by an economic depression:

> Brinton:
>
> The years preceding the outbreak of revolution witnessed unusually serious economic, or at least financial, difficulties of a special kind...and that revolutions often come during economic depressions, which follow on periods of generally rising standards of living."[cxxvi]

Eric Hoffer wrote extensively on the psychology of mass movements after World War II and noted the "new poor" would often be reliable foot soldiers in a revolution.[cxxvii]

Like Brinton, Hoffer theorized mass movements could be triggered by people who had found societal status and then lost it.[cxxviii]

He believed such an event is more likely when the military classes of society are demoralized.[cxxix] In terms of leadership, he maintained the revolutionary leader does not "create the conditions which make the rise of a movement possible," but "once the stage is set, the presence of an outstanding leader is indispensable. Without him, there will be no movement."[cxxx]

Both Brinton and Hoffer believed a successful mass movement required a strong element of hope in conjunction with a clearly defined "evil" or "devil."[cxxxi][cxxxii]

We are not going to assume Brinton and Hoffer had the foresight to predict a twenty-first-century American mass movement. Even Brinton acknowledged, "Revolutions are more remarkable for their differences."[cxxxiii] Though, if we believe human nature is geared to a predictable arc of power and regeneration, these men may offer some clues to our own path forward.

When Americans think of revolutions, they envision the proletariat (working classes) rising and overthrowing the bourgeoisie (wealthy elites). This is due to the overwhelming Marxist bias found at Western universities. But if we look back into history, our first divorce had nothing to do with class envy. The Founding Fathers were not poor when the Revolutionary War broke out. In fact, nearly all those men came from the highest orders of society.[cxxxiv]

Contrary to Marxist logic, a twenty-first-century American mass movement can occur when the wealthy, the skilled working classes, and the military classes align in *hating* the ruling elites.

Moving forward, we will refer to these groups as the *Haves*, *Doers*, and *Warriors*.[cxxxv]

The "Haves" are the millionaires and billionaires who possess the power to fund movements. Amazingly, this group today is nearly split 50/50 between the Democrats and Republicans.[cxxxvi] The "Doers" are the highly skilled men and women in the middle who keep the country running on a day-to-day basis. Without the Doers, we would not have engineers, nurses, programmers, farmers, factory workers, scientists, builders, and the many other highly skilled professions in the private economy. The "Warriors" are our military and law enforcement stewards.

If Crane Brinton and Eric Hoffer are right, the proper elements of hate, hypocrisy, and a *clearly defined devil* are the forerunners in fueling radical societal change.

If we think about it, the left has had their devil for years.

It is us.

We are the imperialists, racists, homophobes, xenophobes, and polluters who are destroying the planet. "We" are the reason why millions of college-educated millennials are willing to ruin their lives to follow someone like Bernie Sanders.

As we consider digging ourselves out of an incredible hole, let's take a moment to think about life after Trump. There will be obvious glee on the left in toppling a "demagogue" who *lied and cheated* his way into the White House.

On our side, however, a Trump exit would lead to a temporary void, and his supporters would feel like they pushed all their chips in and lost.

But this mindset would be a mistake.

Rather than pursuing an aggressive mass-movement mentality, the traditionalist would be shamed into going back to the establishment. Instead of taking the fight directly to the leftist *devils,* we would be watching Republicans like Ben Sasse and Lisa Murkowski discussing in good faith statehood for D.C. and Puerto Rico.

We would essentially be planning our own funeral in *a bipartisan* fashion.

As a *first mass-movement step*, the traditionalist should consider using a Trump loss as an opportunity to walk away from the Republican establishment.

Using a grassroots effort, we would avoid following the same path Nancy Pelosi and Chuck Schumer took when Trump won in 2016. Forget the endless impeachment hearings and the relentless anger. Instead, we should consider the strategic concept of going into a "retrenchment" mode.

What does *retrenchment* imply?

A retrenchment would mean traditional voters would formally walk away from the establishment GOP. And they would return after they repurposed themselves into a unified movement that has the majority power, and conviction, to take the fight directly to their cancel culture foes.

We would allow the Democrats to *temporarily* run the national government while we worked underground to build a new and lasting movement. This type of declaration would represent an astounding moment in American politics. It would be the first time in the US, the people, and *not* the elites, completely overhauled a political party from the ground up.

Under such a retrenchment plan, building a new GOP would be prioritized over stopping progressive overreach in D.C. This concept brings us back to answering a very important question.

Who are we today?

Shouldn't we first answer this question before we begin to worry about who wins the House and Senate in 2022?

Are we the party of fiscal and social conservatives?

Are we the pro-America, pro-worker, pro-business, and anti-swamp *Trump Republicans?*

Or are we the establishment fools who stand by and allow woke Fortune 500 corporations to sell their souls to China and cancel culture?

Our first mass-movement step is about waking up to the reality that we are losing the biggest fight of the twenty-first century.

It doesn't matter that we have two hundred fifty years of historical achievement on our side. The ancient Greeks and Romans were great achievers too.

And both were defeated and thrown into the trash-bins of history.

We are in a deep hole. Like other civilizations before us, we became complacent. We ran up astronomical levels of debt. We lost our edge as a people.

The establishment GOP is not going to ride back onto the scene in Superman-like fashion.

Nor is the media going to expose the intellectual bias of our day. How did today's talking heads get their media *credentials* in the first place? By attending college and sleeping with the devil in our divorce.

The problem for most conservatives is they get complacent with the comfort that comes with obeying rules and following norms. This same dynamic also applies to most military institutions.

How did George Washington use a bunch of undisciplined farmers and laymen to defeat the most powerful army in the world? By stepping beyond established comfort zones and learning the other side's patterns of behavior.

And then by using his adversary's predictability against them.

Assuming we have the better ideas, it is time to step aside and allow D.C., academia, and Hollywood, the real opportunity to show millions of Americans what a progressive utopia would look like under real-world scrutiny.

Just as it is time for us to learn how to exploit incompetence, hypocrisy, and injustice to our mass-movement advantage.

With such an underground strategy, any remaining Republicans in D.C. would join the resistance movement or risk being replaced by it. Traditional voters would still vote to keep *Republicans* in state and local offices—this is not where the true cancer lies. Republican states, and hopefully the Supreme Court, may be helpful advocates should any societal tensions rise to a mass-movement level.

But assuming the conditions were right, we would allow the Democrats to own the federal government without us standing in the way. Instead of trying to be *bipartisan*, the job of any holdover Republicans in Congress would be to expose hypocrisy with an insider's view.

Now, I admit the strategy of allowing the Democrats near-control of the federal government in the short run can be interpreted as political suicide. This type of approach could result in:

- Nationalized health care being established in the US.
- Democrats packing the courts with leftist ideologues.
- Borders opening to millions of undocumented immigrants.
- An accelerating national debt.

It would obviously be gut-check time should any such partisan overreach occur. But what better alternative do we have in our present set of circumstances?

As Donald Trump would say, "What else do we have to lose?"

Why not expose the Democrats' deep dysfunction for all to see while we rebuild and learn how to become an organized resistance movement from the outside looking in?

The kryptonite of the radical left occurs when they are forced to move from revolutionary rhetoric to real-world decision-making. If one wishes to expose the Marxist, cut off a piece of California, Oregon, and Washington and let the do-gooders open their new country to millions of freeloaders.

Or let them raise their corporate tax rate to 90 percent and watch Silicon Valley head for the exits.

Although the media would never say so, the Democrats have bigger problems than the Republicans do. Working-class Democrats are getting squeezed hard by the extreme elements of their party. The Bill Clinton Democrats are close to becoming dinosaurs in this new era of Tlaibs and AOCs.

A Trump exit could represent a tremendous opportunity to turn pain and anger into the first steps of a real mass movement. We messed up in letting things get this far. We exploded the debt and slowly allowed the radicals in academia to take over traditional culture.

Isn't it our turn to demand a new movement that can expose and defeat the stealthy oppressors who have moved into our homes, places of worship, and businesses?

Such a plan would include the following elements:

- Abandoning and/or overhauling of the Republican Party and platform.
- Allowing national Democrats the ability to pass legislation with little to no Republican encumbrance.
- Going underground to develop a bold, twenty-first-century political platform.
- Allowing moderate Democrats and independents a voice at the new table.
- Finding national leaders willing to speak beyond political correctness and establishment-minded politics.

- Planting mass-movement seeds within the US military.
- Recruiting Browns, Blacks, and females to become future resistance leaders.
- Encouraging individual states to initiate "civil disobedience" campaigns against the federal government.
- Creating a level of *anger and discontent* that has the potential to lead to widespread civil unrest.

A Democrat president, in conjunction with a Democrat-led House and Senate, would represent an ideal time for traditionalists to reorganize. Our mass-movement plan would further seek to:

- Pit establishment Democrats against the Bernie Sanders Democrats.
- Develop an "agitation plan" that would seek to expose the new progressive custodians of society.

What is an "agitation plan"?

In a mass-movement context, the *agitation* phase would refer to that defining moment when one side decides to openly fight back against the ruling elites using unconventional tactics. To us, the agitation stage would begin once we break away from the establishment Republicans.

As *professional agitators*, we would consider stepping back to become a *minority influence* in public affairs.

This would mean at the federal level, we would *temporarily* remove ourselves from the societal burden that comes with maintaining law, order, justice, and morality.

As the people of action and common sense, the Haves, Doers, and Warriors have a natural inclination to dismiss bureaucrats, artists, and academics as *nerds on a playground*. We ask ourselves, "How can they be so weird?"

But maybe we should look closer at our own arrogance.

We are close to losing the biggest fight of this century. *The nerds* have nearly won over our kids, the media, and pop culture without firing a shot. What is so crazy about borrowing parts of their playbook and *having a little fun doing so*?

Let's listen to Alinsky:

> Ridicule is man's most potent weapon. A good tactic is one your people will enjoy. If you're not having a ball doing it, there is something very wrong with the tactic.

Hate and right-wing stupidity are not going to change our fate.

But *humor* can.

What are the two traits all extremists share in common?

Arrogance and self-righteousness.

Understanding this reality and exposing the do-gooders with *laughter* may represent the first step in disarming today's thought police.

Moreover, the traditional radical would not want to come out guns-a-blazing after a Trump loss. Yes, time is running out in turning the tables on the woke diehards. And yes, there is nothing funny about the crazies who are close to overturning a global order. But if we don't find the proper blend of humility, patience, and persistence this time around, we will end up following the same marginalized route of the Tea Party.

Let's find perspective in these extraordinary times. Let us provoke, antagonize, and humiliate the other side without taking ourselves so damn seriously.

And then, let's go back to Saul Alinsky for the most important element of an agitation mass-movement strategy:

> For example, since the Haves publicly pose as the custodians of responsibility, morality, law, and justice (which are frequently strangers to each other), they can be constantly pushed to live up to their own book of morality and regulations. *No organization, including organized religion, can live up to the letter of its own book. You can club them to death with their "book" of rules and regulations.*[cxli]

Once the traditionalist truly understands he or she has become the distressed minority, the new ruling elites would be forced to "live up to their own playbook of morality and regulations."[cxlii]

What would the progressive priorities be once they become the official stewards of "responsibility, morality, law, and justice?" Their list would probably look something like this:

- wealth redistribution
- reparation for Blacks
- defunding law enforcement
- a Green New Deal
- nationalized health care
- cutting back on military spending
- climate change
- open borders
- free college for all.

It doesn't take a Saul Alinsky to see how much fun we could have "clubbing them to death" with their own book of rules.

This would mean red states would pick constant fights with the federal government, traditional voters would antagonize liberal elites, and consumers would make companies pay a price for lying in bed with leftist fanatics.

Under such a strategy, we would seek to hold every progressive influencer a hundred percent accountable to their Democrat Socialist playbook.

Look at how effective today's leftists are in bullying companies to achieve political means. As outside agitators, we would turn the tables and learn how to exploit inconsistencies and hypocrisies to our mass-movement advantage.

Just like us, the Democrats are unprincipled. Today's progressive elites are not living in 1,200-square-foot bungalows in low-income areas; they are more likely to own three mansions and have a carbon footprint the size of some small towns.

How did Al Gore make $200 million dollars after he left D.C.?

How did Chelsea Clinton's net worth become over ten million dollars?[cxxxvii]

If Elizabeth Warren supports public schools so much, why did her son attend an elite private school?[cxxxviii]

How did Hunter Biden make millions of dollars in the Ukrainian natural gas industry?[cxxxix] What does Hunter Biden know about natural gas exploration?

And instead of getting angry at Black Lives Matter for demanding reparations, why not allow the Democrats to pass such legislation?

Afterwards, we would ask our Latino and Asian friends what they think of having to pay for such a ridiculous nineteenth-century tab.

Rather than debating why free college would further diminish the value of a college degree, we would stand down and allow Congress to take such a vote.

At the same time, we would be asking the millions of millennials who just paid off their student loans, what they think of free college.

Instead of getting mad at an open-border policy, our border patrol friends would provide cell phone visuals of unaccompanied minors being detained under a Democrat-led presidency.

Let us further our agitation discussion by going back to the reality Asian Americans are voting for Democrats at a nearly 2:1 margin. It is also common knowledge Pacific Rim and Southeast Asian parents value studying hard and getting their children into the best colleges.

In this manic era of trying to push Blacks into every elite university, our billionaire Haves would fund think tanks that analyze the ACT and SAT test results between Asians and Blacks. How many Asian students with a mean ACT score of *32* are losing out to Black students with a score of *18*?

Assuming such disparities exist, shouldn't Asian parents be made aware of the fact that *diversity means more than merit* with most Democrats?

Why should Asian parents encourage their children to study so hard when the end result is already predetermined by a group of social engineers?

Next, let's move over to the billionaires who fund progressive movements. Bill Gates sometimes aligns himself with the Democrats. But Bill also likes to fly in his private jets. Beyond exploiting the hypocrisy of his enormous carbon footprint, we would demand to know why Bill Gates is flying in privilege while the rest of us are sitting in coach.

Personally, I do not care whether Bill Gates travels by private jet or by bicycle. But if Gates wants to interface with the anti-American globalists at the Paris climate accords shouldn't we hold him to the same standards as any other citizen who wishes to travel to France?

Just as we would monitor whether Gates' Board of Director friends at Microsoft are *diverse, inclusive, and accommodating to labor unions.*

As the US continues to politically deteriorate, there are many other fault-lines the Democrats would own once the dumb establishment Republicans are forced to step out of the way.

In this trillion-dollar stimulus era, maybe interest rates will stay low for decades and the politicians can continue to run up enormous annual deficits. But what happens when inflation skyrockets and the Federal Reserve is forced to quadruple interest rates? Who is going to make the hard decisions of curtailing entitlements and raising taxes under such a set of circumstances?

They would.

Just as they would be held responsible for millions of refugees pouring across the border, a stock market crash, five-dollar-a-gallon gas, Antifa uprisings, increased levels of crime, and a financial debt crisis.

I admit, it is terrible having to think this way. But as a country, aren't we traveling down this path already? Why not accelerate the process while there is still time to reverse course?

Should the timing be right, traditional agitators would also consider inciting "illegal" behavior to provoke the ruling classes to either stand down or punish the revolutionaries for *their improper* behavior. Here's Brinton again:

In each revolution, there is a point, or several points, where constituted authority is challenged by the illegal acts of the revolutionists. In such instances, the routine response of any authority is to have recourse to force, police, or military.^{cxlviii}

We are not asking traditional patriots to be lawless thugs. The moronic behavior that happened at the Capitol Building in 2021 played right into the hands of CNN and the New York Times.

Whereas the conservatives of the 1960s used imagery of lawless hippies to be the face of the counterculture, today, the left would love nothing more than for the KKK and QAnon to be the face of our future resistance movement.

We're not looters. We are friends of law enforcement and the military. We are not going to put our friends and allies in awkward situations.

We would instead be calculated and smart in how we break laws, customs, and PC norms.

If these types of mass-movement tactics are done well, the "new custodians" of society would find themselves having to walk the fine line of enforcing their utopian playbooks with apprehension from law enforcement and the military.

In what would essentially become a delicate game of cat-and-mouse, the traditionalist would seek to agitate the do-gooder elites into the unenviable position of having to use an unsympathetic group of Warriors to stop the *illegal* behavior of the Haves and Doers. Then we would seek to exploit any overreactions or underreactions to our advantage.

The *ugly divorce* tactics we are considering will never change the hearts and minds of those brilliant human beings who tie their personal identities to an Ivy League piece of paper.

Nor will we change the minds of the brilliant artists who can vividly dream of the greatest utopia possible to humankind.

But could such strategies allow millions of everyday Americans to experience a brief glimpse of Cuba or Venezuela in their own backyards?

As an organized resistance movement, the traditionalist would aspire to create a level of hatred that would motivate low-information voters to despise the hypocrisy and double standards of the Barack's, Biden's, and Kamala's.

We would coordinate police boycotts in radical blue cities. If someone like Alexandria Ocasio-Cortez sought to disband the police, *we* would begin by asking our police friends to *stay home sick* in her district.

Instead of wasting millions of dollars funding establishment Republicans, conservative billionaires would funnel money to mass-movement patriots.

Rather than remaining guilt-ridden and quiet, traditionalist Doers would use their numbers and influence to ridicule the myriad of woke edicts being handed out at home, in the public schools, and in the workplace.

Just as they would learn how to identify and expose hypocrisy with mayors, city councils, and school boards.

Perhaps most striking, today's Warriors would *contemplate* the unthinkable idea of one day breaking ranks with their woke superiors. No, we're not talking about being an idiot and getting dishonorably discharged from the military. Rather, our enlisted men and women would begin questioning more and more in private why their Commander in Chief is purging patriots and replacing them with incompetent pawns.

The Haves, Doers, and Warriors do not have the structural handicaps the Have-Nots had in the 1960s. Traditionalist agitators could be very creative in how they forced the ruling elites to live up to their own set of rules.

We could accomplish in five years what took the 1960s radicals fifty years to do.

What is the ultimate goal with this *bad divorce* strategy?

- *To create a level of chaos and hypocrisy that would expose today's leftist fanatics in McCarthy-like fashion.*
- *To win today's ideological battle—on our terms.*
- *To build a new and repurposed country, unified beyond race and ethnic origin.*
- *To show the world Americans will use revolutionary tactics to defeat tyranny on its own soil.*

If Hoffer and Brinton are correct, the goal of an agitation movement is to antagonize and expose the other side until their *"prevailing order is discredited."*

I acknowledge this type of revolutionary talk seems unlikely. In addition, there is no guarantee millions of Republican voters would have the patience to see such a plan through.

But if human history has taught us anything, it is the reality that civilizations and borders are in a perpetual state of flux. Should our endless debt and dysfunction continue as a country, how much longer can we wait for the democratic process to heal itself?

Is Thomas Jefferson right—does *the tree of liberty* need to be refreshed every hundred years...?

Moreover, is today the time to stop the crazies before it is too late?

Our strategy of taking the US to the brink would seek to expose the intellectual contagion of our era through tactics of public exposure, personal humiliation, and strategic lawlessness.

At the same time, we would be working underground and around the clock to build a powerful and lasting platform with both Democrats and Republicans.

Would millions of patriots be willing to do what other Americans did before us? Would Republicans *and Democrats* alike be willing to risk personal safety and comfort to rid American society of its *cancel culture devil*?

Our mass-movement gamble is essentially an all-in bet that assumes millions of Americans—and perhaps the military— would eventually join with us if they were presented a stark enough choice between two incompatible views of human nature.

As we move deeper into our *bad divorce* conversation, there is one potential wildcard that may yet enter the discussion:

Is it possible an ex-president Trump could lead a resistance movement from the outside?

Would an ex-Commander in Chief dare ask his military friends to break their code of silence?

Today, we are reluctant to say we support Trump in public. We attend sporting events where athletes kneel and play two national anthems. We also stand down as the namesakes of heroes from the past are knocked down by fanatics.

How long can any civilization disregard its entire past without eventually sabotaging its own future?

At what point will it be time *for us* to make a stand with courage, conviction, and an Alinsky level of organization?

Chapter 12: The Devil and Donald Trump

The quality of the ideas seems to play a minor role in mass movement leadership. What counts is the arrogant gesture, the complete disregard of the opinions of others, the singlehanded defiance of the world.

—Eric Hoffer

Assuming our democratic paralysis continues, could an *ex-president Trump* lead an American mass movement from the outside?

Donald Trump is a transformative leader. This explains why he is allowed so much latitude by his followers. His supporters don't care about all his "lies" and grandstanding. What these millions of Americans desire, is a passionate voice who is willing to take the fight directly to their cancel culture foe.

While a *third* American divorce may seem unlikely, the underlying fault lines may already be in place:

- *Three* impeachments in the last four presidencies.

- There exists a political divide potentially greater than that of the Civil War.
- Progressive overreach in Washington D.C.
- There is a massive accumulation of national debt.
- Unresolved racial tensions.

Would Donald Trump be willing to take the USA to the brink to win today's ideological battle?

And is Trump the *right person* to lead such a movement?

We have learned from Crane Brinton and Eric Hoffer the early stages of a mass movement require patience, discipline, and organized resistance. The broader goal is to agitate, expose hypocrisy, and eventually *discredit* an established ruling order.

Importantly, everyday people must experience real economic pain and loss before they are willing to demand radical societal change.

Let us begin this conversation by assuming Donald Trump re-enters the scene. An agitated-minded Trump would move slow and avoid coming on too strong. Just as he would stop talking about how he lost the 2020 election.

Rather than knocking a feeble Joe Biden at every turn, Trump would allow Americans to *feel* what a progressive presidency means to their everyday lives.

And instead of bragging about past accomplishments, Trump would seek to *chart a hopeful future in the middle of a dark storm.*

This process would begin by going underground and building alliances with powerbrokers in every corner of society including the military.

As a Joe Biden presidency sought to *purge right-wing extremists* from the upper ranks, an ex-president Trump would seek to build alliances with those active- and ex-military influencers who see trouble brewing under a woke military command structure.

Donald Trump would also seek to significantly increase his levels of support with the public. He would begin this process by officially burying the establishment Republicans. This could easily be accomplished by stopping their flow of money and endorsements.

Next, Donald Trump would formally replace the GOP platform with a *Trump doctrine.*

President Trump may not care much for details. Most big-picture leaders don't. But in this game of cat and mouse, details will matter. Instead of speaking in generalities to a sympathetic Fox News host, Trump would convene a convention tasked with building a new Republican manifesto that is *pro-America, pro-worker, pro-business, and anti-swamp.*

This announcement would be made in Trump-like fashion and rallies would be held across the country to create further buzz and excitement. Under such a plan, the best minds from every corner of society would be sought to build a twenty-first-century platform that can best sort out the challenges associated with globalization, big tech, an emerging China, a broken system of education, and an endless debt cycle.

The problem today for both the Democrats and Republicans is that neither party can adequately explain what they stand for. Meanwhile, there are millions of Americans standing in limbo as *political independents.*

Why not use this reality to build a larger coalition of mass-movement support?

A Trump doctrine would also seek to give employees greater rights in the workplace. This takes us back to considering legislative initiatives such as double time wages on Sundays for retail workers, greater 401k matches during profitable years, and outlining a CEO/median pay formula that allows workers to receive a greater share of profits during good years.

From an economic standpoint, a new Trump/Republican platform would seek to move beyond the perception that Republicans only care about rich people. And as labor unions continue to diminish in stature, a Trump doctrine would essentially seek to fill such a void without the corruption and archaic work rules that seem to follow union bosses.

By improving the big-three issues employees care about most—pay, health care, and pensions—a new political platform would seek to cut off the *inequality lifeline* that keeps the AOC's and Tlaib's in the news media cycles.

Moving beyond economics, a Trump doctrine would codify traditional definitions on gender and marriage. In this era of *transgender girls* competing against biological girls in high school sports, are everyday Americans finally moving closer to putting a lid on the *expanding gender galaxy?*

Assuming a comprehensive Trump platform follows the discarded Republican playbook, Asian and Latino Americans would also receive their long-awaited welcome packages in the form of a detailed Trump immigration policy.

Our divorce battle is not going to be won without greater levels of support from Asian and Latino Americans. Most first- and second-generation Asian and Latinos have not yet been polluted by the universities. Their politics and value systems are more likely to align with ours.

It should be an immediate priority for Trump's *insurgent* Republican Party to get today's *twenty-first-century swing voters* onto our team. This would mean Trump would clarify that beyond the *rapists and murderers* there are also millions of great Latino people who are essential to a strong America.

In addition, Trump would clarify that the United States desires more, and not less, talented, hard-working Asians from places like Hong Kong and Taiwan.

As Black and White Americans continue to dumb themselves down with the education of victimology and wokeness, the United States will almost certainly require more highly skilled Doers from Asia and Latin America.

And as China continues to show its true colors, there will be millions of talented human beings who will be willing to *defect* to a re-purposed America.

Such an immigration plan would clarify that divisive ethnic labels like Pacific Islander, Hispanic, non-Hispanic white, African American, and Asian American would no longer show up as census questions. Whether this type of change occurs in the federal bureaucracy, or not, the broader message is that a *new Republican Party* will directly confront the power of identity politics in aggressive fashion.

More importantly, this type of proclamation would seek to unify the country beyond the politics of gender and ethnicity.

Could an ex-president Trump pull off the first stages of a mass movement using patience, specificity, and unification?

Could our ex-president chart a course of hope and opportunity for those millions of Americans who are disconnected from politics?

Assuming so, what would come next?

Beyond formalizing a specific *Trump doctrine*, our ex-president would finally expose the true devil in our divorce story.

And this fight should be taken directly to their front doorsteps. If we want to defeat *our true enemy*, Trump should declare war on academia. He should make his intentions known not as a commencement speaker, but as an outside agitator who knocks down doors.

Hindsight has taught us that Tea Party tactics presented little threat to the college professors. Here is how a group of Tea Party Republicans picketing outside a university would play out in a typical college classroom:

Professor:

All of us have First Amendment rights to protest in the United States. There is a lot of division in America these days. How many of you saw the protesters outside when you were walking to class? Yes, I saw them too. How many of the protesters looked like you? This is a big problem. There is a generational gap between you and them. Many of those folks are angry at you and me, but they came from an era when it was okay for women to be subservient to their husbands. They came from a period when it was acceptable to force Black people to the back of buses. And in their day, if you were born gay, you were out of luck. You would be stuck in the closet without ever being able to realize your true worth and potential as a human being. They have a right to protest, but so do you! Do we want to return to a point in time when being born Brown, Black, female, or LGBTQ—*anything* other than White and male—relegated you to second-class citizenry? This is certainly not the America I want to go back to.

This type of conventional strategy by older, establishment-minded Whites is not remotely adequate in beating the college professors at their own game. Fortunately for us, however, Donald Trump does not use an establishment playbook.

An ex-president Trump could put the professors on their heels with the pure power of personality. Think about having someone like Donald Trump declaring universities should be held financially responsible if a graduate cannot find a job that justifies the cost of college. Think about Trump ridiculing some of the ludicrous classes that are being taught at our finest colleges: History of Surfing, Lady Gaga and the Sociology of Fame, and Tree Climbing.[cxl] And yes, think about Trump holding massive rallies outside the Ivy Leagues.

Crane Brinton discussed the role of intellectuals in a revolutionary context:

> We may say that in a society markedly unstable there seem to be absolutely more intellectuals...bitterly attacking existing institutions and desirous of a considerable alteration of society, business, and government... we may compare intellectuals of this sort to white corpuscles, guardians of the blood stream; but there can be an excess of white corpuscles, and when this happens, you have a pathological condition.[cxli]

America has a pathological condition that originated inside its universities. Until we realize where the mass-movement fight needs to begin, the establishment Republicans are simply grabbing at *ghosts*.

Today, academic freedom has metastasized into academic tyranny.

Donald Trump, Republican governors, and like-minded college administrators should all reign in the monopoly of thought masquerading as an education. In addition, Trump could inspire thousands of students to become classroom agitators.

If we think about it, now is a great time to be a *traditional radical* in a college environment. Confidence in life does not always come from hanging out with the majority crowd. True confidence comes from being around adversity and, more importantly, embracing it. If college professors are the true source of today's tensions, why not *"club them over the head"* with their own book of rules?[cxlii]

As an adult college student, I would ask social science professors how they reconciled their Marxist beliefs to six-figure salaries. Or I would ask them why they would use any type of privately developed medicine if they believed in a government-run system. Or why would they drive gas-burning cars if fossil fuels are ruining the planet. When they asked me follow-up questions, I would sometimes respond, "I'm not sure—don't you think I'm too *privileged* to adequately answer such questions without bias?"

I realize most nineteen-year-old students would be reluctant to use such tactics. But under the right set of circumstances, professors could be forced to "walk on eggshells" every time they step into their classrooms—especially male professors. Depending on how far college agitators want to take things, every progressive male in power could easily be "Kavanaughed."[cxliii]

Did a male college professor ever use his position to have sex with a female student? Did he ever wear blackface to a frat party? What about controversial social media posts and texts from high school or college—were there any signs of male toxicity, xenophobia, or misogyny before he reached his PhD status?

With or without Trump, traditionalist radicals should make life hell on the universities. If the battle lines begin there, why would any Republican (or Democrat) billionaire donate money to their alma maters?

For what—to get their names engraved on a new monument that could easily be torn down by a future generation of radicalized students? Why not instead fund a movement that seeks to expose the anti-American lunacy that originates on college campuses?

Should younger Americans and their parents begin to question the trillion-dollar student debt racket in greater numbers, there exists the possibility the Marxist professors could be squeezed out by the economics they so despise. Fewer students attending college in the soft majors would diminish the power of universities. Just as it is possible a new employer/employee partnership could diminish the power of academia.

Why don't more companies recruit smart and motivated *high school seniors*?

The military has been using this approach for decades. More recently, Tesla's Elon Musk suggested he values "exceptional ability" over a college degree.[cxliv]

If the universities continue to protect their leftist crusaders with impunity, why not bypass the conventional wisdom of college altogether?

"Squeezing" radical college professors from every angle could cut off the money that funds the cancer in our divorce. In addition, putting the mass-movement bullseye on the professors and their enablers in pop culture could result in more *intellectuals* and celebrities finding the confidence to break ranks with their colleagues. Is it possible this type of "transfer of allegiance" could result in another *emperor has no clothes* moment in American society?[cxlv]

Could the agitated-minded traditionalist(s), a new Republican platform, and an aggressive ex-president unmask our devil without having to break up the country?

In this era of critical race theory and wokeness, could an ex-president Trump (and us) defeat the college professors in McCarthy-like fashion?

Or would Trump have to consider the radical idea of moving the divorce battle lines even further?

Using his power to attract immediate media attention, Trump could control the divorce strings like a puppet master. He would seek to make additional friends before declaring war on his enemies. When the timing was right, Trump could agitate the leftist radicals into overplaying their hands as lawless anarchists. And assuming Blacks continue to project a deeper dysfunction onto the police and the entire American founding, Trump could easily incite racial tensions further than they already are today—all while increasing his support levels with more Whites and Browns.

Under a weak Democrat presidency, it is likely angry and emboldened Blacks will overplay their hands. As will groups like Occupy Wall Street and Antifa. The left is not disciplined, organized, or unified by a lasting cause. And they will seek political payback for backing Biden in 2020.

What does this mean to Trump and to us?

It means we are once again moving into the dangerous waters of race in America.

Today, *all* Whites are presumed guilty and privileged without a trial. The Irish, the Italians, the Jews-all of the Americans whose ancestors fought Anglo discrimination in the past have been thrown into the same dirty laundry basket with Christopher Columbus.

Conversely, questioning anything about Black culture has become a major no-no. Forget about the 75% out of wedlock stats, the incarceration rates, and the disproportionate dependence on government.

In this era of guilt and wokeness, *radicalized Blacks and Whites* are willing to destroy every White tradition to promote *tolerance* and *diversity.*

To them, *Make America Great Again* implies a return to a racist past. These Americans do not seem to understand they are throwing away the best set of ideas the world has ever known to pursue a fantasyland.

Just as they don't seem to understand that abandoning men like Jefferson, Washington, and Lincoln will eventually open the doors to tyrants like Lenin, Mao, and Castro.

As we further consider the dynamics of race and revolution, it is perhaps time to ask two very troubling questions:

Can the original sin of slavery be remedied without traditional Whites having to give up who they are?

Does valuing strong families, limited government, and a merit-based economy imply racism?

As an older American who witnessed urban Black culture in real time, maybe I am *racist* beyond repair. Maybe younger Americans have it right and older people like me are on the wrong side of history.

But here is the problem—

Under today's rules, I am not allowed to say anything. I just have to keep my mouth shut and feel guilty. If I say otherwise, my reputation will almost certainly be destroyed.

This type of First Amendment dilemma has major mass-movement implications. How long can the silent majority remain silent?

How long will millions of Americans stand by idle and watch two hundred fifty years of history get washed down the drain?

Eric Hoffer wrote: "Every great cause begins as a movement, becomes a business, and eventually degenerates into a racket."[cxlvi] America was founded on a powerful set of ideas that have been diluted to the point of almost being irrelevant.

The United States has become a *big racket* with nearly everyone taking and few giving back.

Big-business Republicans don't want to rock the boat because they are making money from the trillions of dollars flowing out of D.C. and China.

Democrats are hiding behind the cancel culture extremists because they hate Trump more than they hate the devil who keeps them in office.

Neither party is willing to make difficult choices.

This all perhaps brings us back to our previous *Revolutionary Gamble of the Century* discussion. Is today the time for someone like Donald Trump to promote an Article V convention?

Or is today the time for *us* to step beyond a dysfunctional marriage with clarity, confidence, and a *plan*?

Chapter 13: Taking the USA to the Brink

"The masses go into a revolution not with a prepared plan of social reconstruction, but with a sharp feeling that they cannot endure the old regime."

—Leon Trotsky

As we consider moving our "ugly divorce" conversation into a more specific plan of action, what do we mean when we say, "taking the US to the brink to defeat a leftist cancer?" Are we talking about agitating the country into civil unrest for a couple of months, getting the Marxists to repent, and then lighting up a big victory cigar?

Or are we talking about throwing the United States into years of chaos, violence, and potential for great loss of life?

In the long arch of history, the Revolutionary and Civil Wars are regarded as *positive* events that changed the course of mankind. Nonetheless, thousands of people died, families suffered great losses, and the dark side of humanity was revealed to millions of human beings.

If the American way of life were to be challenged by a foreign adversary, most of us would be willing to pick up arms immediately to defend our country. But *today's enemy* may be a family member or a good friend whom we have known for years.

As we try to navigate these difficult waters, the first question we must ask ourselves again is: what is our mass-movement objective?

What are we trying to accomplish with this book?

Sure, our overreaching theme is about defeating the devils of relativism, globalism, and Marxism. But what do these abstract concepts mean to the average person?

This book is about realizing a misguided group of elites have too much power over the voting masses. Today's intellectuals and bureaucrats have put an entire global order in great peril. Using soft tactics, hard tactics—and even the risk of a geographical breakup—our primary objective is to ferment a mass movement that is powerful enough to expose and defeat the intellectual classes of society. Ultimately, our "revolutionary gamble" is about radically transforming academia and the federal bureaucracies.

Can we trigger a democratic reboot by "suffocating" the cancer in our marriage?

Our political tensions did not originate in living rooms or in corporate boardrooms; nor were our societal fault lines hatched in Moscow, Beijing, or Tehran. Words and phrases like equity, social justice, critical race theory, and white privilege were developed here, right in our own backyard.

The swamp has simply grown out of control. Look at what happened to Donald Trump shortly after he took over the White House in 2017. Throughout Trump's presidency, all we heard from the mainstream media was centered around "Russian collusion." Forget the fact that once Trump left office, the entire collusion narrative was shown to be a hoax perpetuated by anti-Trump operatives working inside the government.

What should have been exposed as the biggest attempted coup in our nation's history was simply buried and swept under the rug by the so-called stewards of democratic values. How many media outlets renounced the fact that they were peddling fake news to millions of voters throughout an entire presidency?

How many subversive operatives were thrown in jail?

I'm not sure *the average person* is remotely close to understanding the real stakes in this revolutionary showdown. We've become a dumb and aloof country. China already knows this. Just as they understand that ignorance at a majority level is the precursor to a failed democratic state. In this sense, it may only be a matter of time before the concept of "ugly" reaches our shorelines.

How can we motivate the average voter to realize a small group of highly educated crazies are destroying the best social compact available to mankind? Can a new Republican Party break today's gridlock? Can we achieve our mass-movement goals by "retrenching" and changing the conversation inside the marriage? Or do we have to consider the risks associated with blowing up the status quo to create real societal change?

In all honesty, the answer to these questions may be "all of the above."

We now understand from Crane Brinton and Eric Hoffer what fuels radical societal change—*hatred of the ruling elites, hypocrisy, inept governance, a demoralized military, economic hardship and unfair taxation, and an over-abundance of intellectuals attacking existing institutions.* If we were to begin checking boxes, we are already in a revolutionary danger zone. And if we look back at the mistakes of the Romans and Greeks, there are other boxes that can be checked—unsustainable levels of debt, moral decadence, weak leaders, political instability, outstretched armies, lack of assimilation, and division between the ruling elites. If there were to be a color-coded revolutionary scale, America is probably somewhere between orange and red as a country.

In this fragile democratic environment, it would not be difficult for an organized group of Haves, Doers, and Warriors to agitate the United States into a state of societal chaos. Just as an insurgent mass-movement leader may be able to instigate pockets of the military to temporarily set aside their enlistment oaths. If thousands of uniformed personnel are already willing to give up their ranks and privileges to avoid a vaccination, there are fault lines brewing inside today's military.

In these treacherous times, we need to better understand ourselves and our enemy. As the people of action, the revolutionary-minded Haves, Doers, and Warriors are at an immediate disadvantage to the bureaucrats, artists, and intellectuals. Our adversary is patient; we are not. Give us a task and a deadline and we'll get the job done. They, on the other hand, are accustomed to the slow and deliberative movement that occurs in the halls of academia and government.

In the initial stages of a movement, we can't be impulsive and reckless. The stakes are simply too high. A repeat of *January 6* could set us back years. Instead of charging up hills with muskets, our first mass-movement steps are about winning hearts and minds. Our initial tactics are more about understanding human psychology than they are about putting a revolutionary manual together, acting on it, then finding our happy place. Before there was a George Washington, there were years of British overreach that "touched men's souls." And before there was an Abraham Lincoln, there existed decades of stench from the original sin of slavery.

I acknowledge how fun it would be to beat the Democrats in the next election.

But any such pleasures will be short-lived until we expose, discredit, and reform academia. Our problems as a democracy are not going to change until education as we know it today is radically reformed from top to bottom. From preschool to graduate school, our schools and universities must be turned upside down to defeat the devil of our era.

What good is it to focus on putting Republicans in office, while the academics continue to poison millions of minds with impunity? Is a Republican majority in Congress going to change the radicalization process playing out at our colleges and in our public schools?

Is a Republican-led Congress and a Democrat-controlled presidency going to drain the swamp that grew inside academia but has since spread into government, the media, and big tech?

Today's problems originated in the 1960s. Putting Republicans in office may feel good for the moment, but this approach hasn't done anything to defeat a disease that has been brewing for decades. In this sense, we have become the greyhound dog that chases the mechanical rabbit not realizing we won't ever catch up to the target.

As previously discussed, *our first mass-movement step* is about walking away from the establishment Republicans and *retrenching* as a people. This symbolic move will prepare us for any significant change that may be lying on the horizon. Just as it is about finding the courage to walk away from a once-strong friendship that has since grown sour.

Our second mass-movement step is about putting the best minds together to formulate a new Republican manifesto. This move is about telling ourselves, our friends, and our enemies who we hope to be. It is about informing us and others that we will no longer tolerate the abuse and the anger.

With or without Trump, now is the time to refine our mission statement of who we are today and who we want to become tomorrow.

Importantly, our new platform can't be formulated to just win the next election—it must be constructed to show what America will look like for the rest of this century and beyond. Yes, we will articulate our pro-America, pro-worker, pro-business, and anti-swamp vision in further detail. But we also need to think longer. If our problems as a country are ultimately rooted in philosophy, we need to set our sights beyond economics and domestic policy. We need to include men like Locke, Hobbes, Hume, and Montesquieu in our next *Great Conversation.*

Let's assume freewill in the human order is limited to a repetitive path of birth, decadence, and regeneration. While in college, the professors would refute this premise by inferring my reasoning was biased from a Judeo-Christian upbringing. But let's set them aside for a moment and bring Moses and Socrates back into the conversation.

If we think about things, the United States is likely following a very similar path to that of ancient Greece and Rome. Today's progressives are yesterday's pagans. As to us...we are the descendants of a great set of ideas that are being drowned out by debt, identity politics, unenforced borders, and moral decay.

Instead of being mindful of the seven deadly sins, our moral focus is more about discovering psychological self-actualization. Today, the stoic Navy SEAL is considered toxic and narcissistic. Conversely, the genderqueer who has found inner peace with *their* therapist has become a societal rockstar.

We know we can't continue going down this road as the defender of the free world. And yes, we know the progressives will eventually eat their own. By placing the inherently flawed human being at the center of their Marxist universe, it will only be a matter of time before self-indulgence and the politics of envy self-implode.

Our second mass-movement step is about demanding a *Great Discussion* on not only what it means to be a Republican, but more importantly, what it means to be a human being in the twenty-first century. In such a setting, everything should be on the table to contrast ourselves not only with the leftist college crusaders but also the emergence of a Chinese giant that hopes to put the final dagger into Western civilization.

By thinking on a longer time horizon than winning the next election, we would be banking on the reality that the masses will one day realize progressive utopias like California are destined to become moral wastelands of criminal behavior and central planners run amok.

We would be playing a long game in defining who we are with the hope that others will eventually pick us over them. Just as we would be willing to lose elections in the short run to get back to who we once were.

Our third mass-movement step is about declaring that we will no longer speak the language of our angry partner. This means, in a very specific way, that we are done speaking their language and living in their reality of hate and envy. Buzzwords like microaggressions, safe spaces, xenophobia, racism, privilege, and equity would thus be banished from the dinner table. Instead, we would go back to our roots with confidence and declare life will never be equal and free. Just as we will reiterate that the human existence should be measured by equality of opportunity, and not equality of outcome.

These types of distinctions in words may not sound revolutionary, but they are. Having a real debate about *outcome versus opportunity* goes to the very heart of why we are so close to a societal divorce.

Words shape our reality. Using one such example, years ago, I decided to bring Saul Alinsky into my hiring process. Any leader understands the power that comes with team chemistry. I knew from my college experience that mixing *highly educated* employees with *less educated* employees would eventually create unnecessary tensions in the workplace.

So, I made a business decision. I decided I was going to use *their words* to flush out any potentially woke job applicants.

In important job interviews, I would ask prospective employees questions like: *How important is diversity to a company?* The "uneducated employees" were more likely to dance around the question, and say something like this: *"Yes, diversity is important, but I also want to have a chance to grow inside a company that values merit too."*

With the "highly educated employees" I would use the same question and closely observe their body language. In nearly every case, this group of applicants would sit up in their chairs beaming with confidence. This type of question was in their academic wheelhouse, and their ensuing response resonated with who they had become after being indoctrinated at college.

Ironically, it was usually the White—not the Black or Brown applicants—who were most enthusiastic to talk about diversity, social justice, and equity in the workplace.

Once any such interview came to an end, I could predict with near certainty what employees I *wasn't* going to hire. Instead of dealing with EEOC lawsuits, and unnecessary employment litigation, our company was able to focus on winning and sharing the spoils from business success as one united team.

Let's use another example to understand how impactful words can be. *Affirmative action* is obviously a progressive buzzword in most college classrooms. After losing one such classroom debate on the topic, I decided to change my approach the next time the issue came up in class again.

I made the decision to move away from Romney and over to Schumer. When the topic returned several classes later, I scanned a classroom that included a mix of Black, Asian, and White students. This was a smaller, informal class setting, so I had learned beforehand that several of the Black students had attended prestigious private high schools and came from upper-income families. The Whites and Asians appeared to come from mostly lower/middle-income households.

Instead of speaking in Republican platitudes, I reversed course and asked the professor how fair it was that Black students with wealthy parents should be prioritized over those White and Asian students whose parents are not as well-off.

Using their words and logic, I was essentially asking why affirmative action is based on race in lieu of socioeconomic status. I put the "privileged" Black students on the defensive while energizing the White and Asian students.

I used *their* language of identity politics to create a real debate instead of using stale Republican talking points that would have bored the entire class into thinking about their next classroom break.

When another discussion in class moved to the Washington Redskins doing a name change because the word "Redskins" was deemed offensive, I asked why Harvard and Yale shouldn't be included in this discussion too. Weren't these universities built from the blood money of slavery? Isn't today the time to remove the words Yale, Harvard, and any other such namesakes from buildings, resumes, and diplomas?

We know the answer to this question. Forcing the devil to give up those pieces of paper would be akin to asking us to give up our firstborn child. But these tactics are effective. And they can spread like wildfire. Once arrogance and hypocrisy are exposed, everyone will want to pile on and join in on the fun.

Our third mass-movement step is ultimately about seeking *new leaders* who understand the power of words. We need to replace the establishment Republicans with insurgent candidates who have the confidence and ability to redirect the conversation of woke to a real discussion about who we really are as human beings.

Can we expose our devil with a newfound confidence in who we want to be?

Can we peel away millions of common-sense Democrats from their "Democratic Socialist" brethren by using the soft tactics of words?

I admit, these first three steps should be considered low-hanging fruit. But as it stands today, Donald Trump is the only one willing to do any of the heavy lifting. Trump is the only person willing to change the tone in the conversation. Just as he is the last person standing in the way of those timid establishment Republicans who want to quietly blend in and hope "everything will return to normal through the democratic process."

Trump just needs to find the right people to have our Great Discussion, and the first mass-movement table will be set.

Just as we need to do more than attend Trump rallies and tell him how much we love him—it's time for us to get into this game of revolutionary poker.

Out with the old Republican playbook and in with the new…

Redefining who we want to be and how we talk…

Canceling their words, logic, and reasoning from our everyday existence…

Could a weak Biden and a *new way of doing business* be the antidote to our democratic problems? This goes back to our *Chapter 9* ideas about a new Republican Party. Today, millions of Americans are voting with their feet and leaving blue states and cities in droves. Could the combination of *inept governance* and the *promise of a hopeful future* rescue our democracy without the pretext of unwanted chaos?

Or should we up the pressure by adding in the ugly divorce tactics from Chapter's 11 and 12? How much of Saul Alinsky do we want to mix in with Aristotle and Jesus?

Assuming human beings are creatures of habit, it takes a lot to move people out of their comfort zones. Any good coach, general, or CEO can easily explain the risks that come with getting too comfortable in a group setting.

In this sense, the masses are like sheep. And they will only run to a new meadow when they see the wolf.

How do we get the *sheep*, that is, millions of American voters, to move outside their political comfort zones? How do we elevate the passions in the marriage to where the masses will demand radical alterations to society?

Let's begin this discussion by moving into our first hypothetical.

As a *possible fourth mass-movement* step, should we *intentionally allow* the voters to have more uninterrupted time with Joe and Kamala? Look at how inept the government has been in dealing with the COVID-19 pandemic. Who today would fully trust Biden, Harris, Fauci, or the CDC on getting reliable medical advice? When the *real science* catches up to what we are doing right and wrong today, everything we think we know about the virus is probably more wrong than right. Six feet social distancing? Probably wrong. Natural immunity only lasting ninety days? Already proven wrong. True effectiveness of masks? Probably very little. Keeping kids out of school? A tragic mistake that should have never occurred.

With the incompetence of the government on full display, a myriad of low-information voters today *hate* their elected elites. Look at how many apolitical Americans are simply ignoring the CDC recommendations. Look at how many first responders and military people are ignoring their president.

This type of hate, awareness, and *hypocrisy* is exactly what we are trying to ferment on a much larger scale. We know that exposing "the hypocrisy of the ruling elites" is a precursor in discrediting "their prevailing order." Asking us to mask up and stay indoors while they attend an unmasked gala at Barack Obama's sixtieth birthday party? This level of hypocrisy plays right into our mass-movement playbook.

By not having any Republicans to blame, Biden cannot hide, and he must assume full responsibility for the incompetence occurring inside *his* federal government. The question we must ask ourselves today, is how much rope do we give Biden as he moves deeper into his presidency?

Should we consider the radical idea of sitting out future congressional election(s)?

I admit, this potential idea seems laughable at first glance. An *insurgent Republican-controlled House and Senate* could use their investigative powers to wreak havoc and exploit hypocrisy on Biden and the Democrats. But are the Republicans smart enough to keep proper distance from perhaps the worse president in the history of the country? Can we trust *them* to be agitators from the inside? Or will they go back to being establishment buffoons who get blamed for Biden's incompetence?

Republican voters understand how important the right to vote is. For us, waiting outside in the long lines is about respecting those Americans who have fought, and died, for our way of life. To the progressive elites, however, the voting process has become a mere inconvenience that can be manipulated by going door to door and making sure millions of "disenfranchised Americans" *received their ballots in the mail. Oh, and for good measure, personal instructions and a #2 pencil are also provided in how to mark a Democrat straight ticket box. And don't forget to sign the bottom of the ballot...*

Is this what the Founding Fathers envisioned in the 1770s? Are we going to beat the enemy of our day by being conventional? Or are we better off sitting out any federal election that features a RINO Republican on the ballot?

I have no idea how far this book will go, or whether there is enough time for Republicans to boycott the next election cycle. And, in all honesty, this tactic could easily change based on the circumstances occurring on the ground. But make no mistake, organizing millions of voters to stage a massive sit-down would radically change the conversation in our marriage.

Unlike the Democrats, our side is informed enough to pull off such a crazy strategy. We don't need a Stacey Abrams going door to door to get our message out. We would essentially manipulate our own democracy to make the statement that we are done putting establishment enablers in office. Additionally, we would seek to put a magnifying glass on the leftist crazies who are using Biden as their puppet.

Should such a tactic be considered in this toxic environment? Could we expose the other side's "prevailing order" further by putting a weak Biden under a bigger spotlight, while we agitate from the outside?

Whether we sit out an election or not, tactics must be fluid to the situation at hand. "Agitation" must be unpredictable and unrelenting. Once we decide to become full-time agitators, we can't let off the gas just because a particular strategy doesn't go as planned. In addition, tactics should be proportional to the events playing out on the ground. We don't want to overreact and/or underreact to mass-movement opportunities.

The Haves, Doers, and Warriors are smart and organized. Once *we* learn how much fun it is to expose hypocrisy, we can easily ask others to join in on the fun. Recently, liberal celebrities have gone public with their disdain of cancel culture. Comedians are especially intuitive to the dark side of human nature. Democrats like Bill Maher and Steve Harvey are beginning to see the darkness that follows wokeness. Why not partner with such societal influencers? Could we initiate Brinton's *transfer of allegiance* by joining forces with commonsense Democrats? Could we influence pockets of Hollywood and the media to turn on our woke devil? Could our tactics embolden more math and science intellectuals to turn on their humanities and social science brethren?

As outside agitators, we must also understand the distinction between a Nancy Pelosi and an Alexandria Ocasio-Cortez. As much as this may be hard to swallow, Pelosi is not our devil. While she would never say so publicly, she loathes the new millennial "Squad" members almost as much as we do. Pelosi is simply a mouthpiece for the millions of Democrat voters who were radicalized at college or for those victim classes who have succumbed to identity politics and free money. If she were to talk any other way, she would almost certainly lose her political power.

The mainstream Democrat is not our enemy outside of political theater. It is very important we draw this line as we consider moving into our "retrenchment period." Rather, our focus should be on the Marxist-inspired radicals who have found their way inside government and academia. Their belief systems are weighted by Marxist theory that can easily be exposed to the masses. How does an AOC respond to higher crime levels in her district when she believes the police are the problem? How does a Tlaib respond to open border questions when she believes seven billion people should all be part of the same global family?

The bigger microphone the leftist crazies have, the more *sheep* we can move to our side. This explains why our Haves, Doers, and Warriors should consider a *hands-off* approach in congressional districts that elect the most radical of Democrats. Let them live in their intellectual wastelands without any of our help. The more these cities (and states) are run unencumbered by the progressive crazies, the easier it will be for us to show future contrast.

Making alliances with former foes to expose our cancer culture devil...

Applying constant pressure on the universities, D.C., the media, Hollywood, and woke companies...

Considering radical measures such as sitting out congressional elections...

Backing away from deep blue cities and states...

What comes next in this fragile democratic environment? Is there another hypothetical mass-movement tactic that can expose our devil in greater detail?

Let's assume we have defined who we want to be with a new platform, Trump is in or out as the wildcard, and the dysfunction in the country is growing. Instead of attracting more people to our side, though, America remains at a 50/50 political stalemate. Using this set of circumstances, let's discuss the pros and cons of a second hypothetical scenario.

Is it time for us to publicly put a geographical breakup on the table?

Should Trump or some other insurgent-minded Republican float the idea of an Article V convention?

Whether an actual breakup occurs or not, this tactic is akin to one side of a broken marriage finding the courage to put the *d-word* on the table. Could merely talking about a divorce in public fashion avert an actual breakup? Could we create an *us-or-them* moment by suggesting that we want the *swamp officially drained* or we're out of the marriage?

It is acknowledged the America of today is not the America of 1860. Any future breakup would not have contiguous borders like the North and South had. Even the state of Texas is a 55/45 percent red/blue state by political affiliation.

And unlike the 1860s, the Americans of today would not have the stomach for the levels of violence that occurred back then. In addition, we are much more connected via technology. The progressive voter of today who got stuck in a new Red America could still work from home remotely.

While however tempting, now is not the time for *us* to go further down the road of *geographical what-ifs*. Instead, our elite Warriors and Haves should be the ones who *soon* begin the process of putting together a logistical and geographical blueprint for a two-America solution.

Our first matter of business rather, is about getting the message out that things need to change inside the marriage, or we want out. Whether the convention idea occurs or not, this tactic is about upping the ante in declaring that if things don't change soon, we're going to visit an attorney's office.

Let's think about this approach in greater detail. Using our "sheep" analogy, the voting masses would see *two wolves* approaching their grazing meadow. Once we begin talking about an Article V convention in public fashion, the Democrats would immediately paint us as right-wing crazies who want to hurt and kill all the sheep. We, of course, will rely on a written platform to define our future intentions.

Which way will the sheep run?

For the sake of discussion, let's assume thirty-four states do find a way to convene a convention. Further, let's assume both sides try to negotiate a peaceful geographical breakup in good faith. How long would any future Blue America last before their core constituency of socialists, anarchists, and victim classes self-imploded?

While *they* may think we are irrational fools for taking the United States to the revolutionary brink, they would be the ultimate fools to begin a new Blue America under the leadership of Buttigieg, Tlaib, and Newsome.

We hold most of the cards in this dysfunctional marriage. Let the liberal talking heads continue blabbering about the difference in GDP between red and blue states. We bring much more to the marriage than they do, and they know it.

What are we trying to accomplish with tactics like sitting out elections and putting a real geographical breakup on the table?

This controversial question takes us back to the original sin of slavery and Donald Trump.

It is amazing today's NBA is an active business partner with China. Useful idiots who use Marxist themes like social justice are partnering with a slave nation in the twenty-first century. How is what the Chinese are doing with the Uyghurs today any less repulsive than what was happening four hundred years ago in Africa?

As the NBA marches forward with its "equality" campaigns, they are in bed with perhaps the most egregious violator of human rights in the world. God bless those handful of NBA players who recognize the hypocrisy and power grab that accompanies the "End Racism" slogans showing up on the back of their game jerseys.

What is going on today with race is ultimately a power grab; more specifically, a Marxist power grab. Slavery is the ultimate vehicle from the past that keeps ninety percent of Blacks loyal to the Democrat Party. By creating a paradigm of the oppressed and the oppressor, radicalized groups that didn't have the power of the White male yesterday, want instant equality of outcome today. They are willing to destroy everything to capture what they didn't have two hundred years ago.

We are not going to move forward as a unified country without tackling the issue of slavery. That is, unless we fully renounce who we are, and submit to the *new Master*. In this sense, traditional Americans would be forced to follow the path of the South African Whites from the last century. Although the circumstances are different, any such unconditional repentance from us could land us where South Africa finds itself today—a beautiful and abundant nation plagued by corruption, homicides, and Whites fleeing the country.

A once-proud country where the Haves and Doers are being fleeced and murdered for the sins of the past.

Are cancel culture and backdoor Marxism passing fads that can be eradicated with a new Republican playbook and a new conversation?

Or is today the time to prepare ourselves for an unpredictable geographical breakup?

As we try to circle around these types of life-changing questions, let's look at one last hypothetical.

Let's assume our Article V state-sponsored convention idea goes viral.

Let's further assume the economy is tanking, China has taken over Taiwan, crime is out of control, and Biden and Kamala are back in hiding.

Using this type of scenario, we would first seek to revisit Brinton's and Hoffer's revolutionary checklist:

- *Hatred and hypocrisy of the ruling elites*
- *Inept governance*
- *Economic hardship followed by rising standards of living*
- *A demoralized military*
- *Out of control intellectuals*

We should know this list of revolutionary prerequisites by now. If someone like Trump initiated an Article V discussion when inflation was going down and the stock market was going up, he would be playing a dead hand of mass-movement cards. He would not only look like an idiot with the Democrats but also with many of us.

Let's assume, though, that Biden's presidency is a mess, and each of the above boxes are ready to be checked off. Further, Trump is still in the game and is ready to gamble with the future of our country.

What could we anticipate if Trump were to visit the campus of Harvard to advance the radical idea of a two-America solution?

The leftist media would chastise him as a fascist dictator. Then they would provide every reason why a geographical breakup would be a disaster. Social Security and Medicare would be lost; foreign enemies would be emboldened; banks would close; food shortages would ensue. The list goes on and on.

We know what they would do. Just as we know Republican establishment figureheads like Bush and Cheney would declare Trump an enemy to the Constitution.

But what would 330 million Americans think?

More importantly, could this type of scenario have the power to expose and defeat a Marxist disease that not only ails America but also much of Europe, Canada, and Australia?

By taking the country to the brink, would we be willing to risk a geographical breakup to radically upend academia, public education, and the federal bureaucracies?

Moreover, could a new and *Great Discussion* have the power to restore intellectual sanity and the Socratic method back to Western life?

By taking the United States of America to the edge of a revolutionary cliff, could *we*—just as other Americans did two hundred fifty years ago—trigger a democratic rebirth in the West?

Or will both sides harden their positions in passive-aggressive fashion and await to see what happens next?

In 2013, Detroit became the largest US city to declare Chapter 9 bankruptcy.[cxlix] This was a shock to the thousands of people who never contemplated a scenario in which basic services and pension commitments could be wiped away at a moment's notice. The Michigan governor had to appoint a single, unelected official to completely clean house.

An *emergency manager* had arbitrary power to void retirement plans, union contracts, public education compacts, and even decisions made by an active and elected city council.

For nearly two years, a major American city lost its democratic rights.

The emergency manager had the power to give "haircuts" to nearly every financial stakeholder. The problems were so deep, *a dictator* was essentially required to restore order to nearly every facet of life in Detroit.

With Detroit's bankruptcy, everyone initially complained about the haircuts:

- the voters
- the bond holders
- the pensioners
- and the elected City Council.

Thousands of people were angry that a governor and an emergency manager could have so much arbitrary power in a democratically bound city. There were protests. There were racist insults hurled at the Republican governor who *dared* to interfere in Detroit's business. But in the end, everyone got over things, and the books were balanced in Detroit.[cl]

What does Detroit mean to our discussion today?

It may be possible that it is too late to "remedy" the debt and division in the United States.

Like Detroit, the US may one day require its own *emergency manager* to fix the broken democracy that we today call the United States of America.

Chapter 14: An American Dictator

If you know the enemy and know yourself, you need not fear the result of a hundred battles. If you know yourself but not the enemy, for every victory gained you will suffer a defeat. If you know neither the enemy nor yourself, you will succumb in every battle.
—*Legendary Sun Tzu*

Whether Donald Trump remains in our divorce conversation or not, there exists a chance the United States will need to *temporarily* set aside its Constitution. If the US doesn't solve its dual problems of debt and dysfunction in a relatively short order of time, Americans from both the left and right may eventually demand a dictator, autocrat, or *emergency manager* to completely clean house and balance the books.

This is who we are as human beings; and this is what the academic elites don't seem to understand about human nature. Everyone loves freedom when things are going well, but when presented a choice between chaotic freedom or orderly governance, people will eventually choose order over freedom—even if it means compromising civil liberties in the short run.

No one wants to see a dictator in America, but this discussion brings us back to perhaps the three most important questions in the book:

- Under what set of circumstances would the US military break its nonpartisan ranks to lead a reboot of a dysfunctional and broken American democracy?
- At what point would the public be willing to consider its own emergency manager to fix the dysfunction in Washington, D.C?
- If the US broke into two countries, which *side* would the military *align* with?

This last question may be the most important of all. Should blue- and red-Americans not find a way to come together soon, the final arbiter of truth and justice may reside in the Pentagon. The US military has contingency plans for every type of existential threat. Not only are they the best in the world at conducting war, they are also the most respected institution because they do their job well and avoid political gamesmanship.

But have our military elites ever contemplated the logistical, political, and cultural ramifications of a *domestic divorce*?

While I don't have an insider's view, I suspect our military leaders understand the future ramifications associated with a broken democracy in conjunction with an emerging China. And if what I witnessed as a military sub-contractor is playing out on the battlefield, the fanatical bureaucrats and PC police are destroying the Warrior spirit.

By the end of my contracting career, I couldn't handle the nonsense that came with procuring and managing military work: finding opportunistic minority firms to partner with, the endless bureaucracy, and the rampant political correctness. It was as if completing a job the right way was of least priority.

Everything seemed to be about satisfying the PC bureaucracy.

If what I personally experienced working on the military bases here at home is happening in real combat situations, at what point does a decorated group of patriots start asking some hair-raising questions:

- Is the US democracy broken beyond repair?
- What would be the national security ramifications if the United States broke into two separate countries?
- Assuming the country broke into two nations, which side would control the nuclear arsenal?

During the Civil War, military men who fought together for years broke ranks to join the Confederate and Union armies. Would such a repeat set of circumstances play out in a *second civil war*? Or would an overwhelming majority of the military align with *red* over *blue*?

How could anyone high up the military chain of command call themselves a Democrat today?

We are no longer talking about the era of the Andrew Jackson and Harry S. Truman Democrats. We are living in an era where the progressive core values are based on a world without borders, police, and nation-states.

How can active military commanders align with the leftist crazies without first having to *hate themselves*?

How many more monuments of Grant and Lee (and Jackson and Truman) must be destroyed before some very important people break their code of silence?

At what point will the Haves, Doers, and Warriors realize they have the power and numbers to stop the victim classes and anarchists before it is too late?

And at what point will the merchant and the Marine align and say, "Enough is enough?"

We don't have the answers to some very important mass-movement questions. We can only speculate that if things got *ugly*, most military elites would align with a *Red America*. To what extent, we don't know. But if this assumption is wrong, our entire mass-movement strategy could come crashing down. Let's listen to Crane Brinton on how important the military is to a revolutionary movement:

> No revolutionists have ever succeeded until they got a predominance of effective armed forces on their side. This holds true from spears and arrows to machine guns and gas, from Hippias to Castro.[cli]

We learned from Trump's experiment of bringing Democrat generals into the White House that military valor doesn't always translate into seeing the whole battlefield. Thus, there exists the chance the military could align with a future Blue America.

If this type of outcome were to be verifiable, the traditionalist patriot should consider standing down and aborting any plans for a future mass movement. If Brinton is right about the revolutionary significance of the military, it is therefore possible the outcome of any *ugly divorce* could be a predetermined defeat.

We can't be sure if our future mass-movement leader would come from the military, or the civilian world, but in the context of a revolutionary environment, this individual would have to command a level of insight, diplomacy, and leadership that is perhaps only found on a once-every-hundred years basis. In what would have to be an impeccably timed decision, this next George Washington or Abraham Lincoln would have to contemplate moral and political dilemmas no less profound than what occurred in the 1770s and 1860s.

According to Eric Hoffer, it would be around this time the "active stage" of the movement would begin. To the public, the *active stage* could be thought of as that succinct "Boston Tea Party" moment when the masses "kick the bums out" and start over. Unlike the agitation period of a mass movement, which can go on for years, the active stage should be short and concise.[clii] As Hoffer explains, "No mass movement, however sublime its fate and worthy in purpose, can be good if its active stage is overlong..."[cliii]

This logic makes sense. If there were to be a radical transfer of power to a temporary dictator, Americans would never tolerate an open-ended "dictatorship." They would want to know what the *undemocratic* plan is, how long it will take, and how much pain there will be. And unlike citizens of most other countries, we would hold onto our guns throughout the entire process.

During the active phase of a revolutionary environment, the *temporary dictator* would seek to meet with every aggrieved group: Blacks, Browns, Whites, Republicans, Democrats, business and industry, unions, the universities, and many others. And just like the Detroit bankruptcy in 2013, a team of CPAs and auditors would comb through every dollar of federal debt and future financial obligation.

In the best of outcomes, "haircuts" would be given across the board, new coalitions would form, and the country would be put back onto a stable political and financial footing.

In the worst of circumstances, unpredictable violence, forced relocations of millions of people, and new borders would be possible.

Under both paths, every fault line would be under review including race relations, voting rights, citizenship, taxation, debt, bloated bureaucracies, the environment, education, and the specific terms of a possible geographical breakup.

But what about foreign policy? Would countries like China and Iran be able to capitalize off a broken United States?

This question leads us to one last fault line. Eric Hoffer wrote that the ideal, mass-movement "devil" is a foreigner.[cliv] Should a country like China overplay its stealth intentions, is it possible America could finally find a catalyst powerful enough to unite blue- and red-Americans? Let's listen to Hoffer:

> Common hatred unites the most heterogeneous elements. To share a common hatred, with an enemy even, is to infect him with a feeling of kinship, and thus sap his powers of resistance.[clv]

The Western elites were wrong in assuming a market-reformed China would naturally merge into a democracy. Politicians on both sides are scrambling to catch up to the reality that the US and China may be heading on a future collision course. Nearly two-thirds of the public now have an unfavorable view of China.[clvi] Each day, more and more of us are waking up to the possibility of a clash of civilizations.

Are human beings better served with the fast-moving hand of a Chinese autocrat? Or is the slow and sometimes inefficient self-governance style of the Americans the gold standard in human affairs? In a healthy and vibrant society, these types of questions would have already been debated at our universities. Yet in this era of one-sided intellectualism, these types of inconvenient questions go against the prevailing progressive wisdom that *human beings are getting closer to embarking on a future path of global harmony.*

Should China or another hostile adversary provoke the United States at a time of crisis, could Americans come together like they did after 9/11/2001? Possibly. But probably not for long. It is difficult to come together with a partner who hates everything about their original wedding vows. After 9/11, I paid close attention to the professors, and it was almost as if they were happy *America got what it deserved.*

How can there be any future reconciliation when one side of the marriage has so much hatred for its holidays, monuments, and traditions?

I really don't want to suggest this next thought, but does the possibility exist the "American Way" could one day lose out to the "Chinese Way"? Today, autocrats in countries like China look at our dysfunction and say to their masses, "Look how bad and inefficient the Western democracies are."

And at this moment in time, the Chinese are *correct* in their observations.

In the long run, however, there is no way an autocratic civilization can compete against another way of life that attracts people with benevolence.

How long can nine men play the shell game of painting individual liberty, freedom of the press, and due process as a bad thing?

Only as long as the United States remains a divided and dysfunctional country.

In this sense, a *healthy United States* will always pose an existential threat to the Politburo and other dictatorships like it. To keep their power in the long run, the Chinese elites need us to be more dysfunctional than they are. This may explain why their government plants spies in our colleges.[clvii]

The Chinese want to assist the *American* professors in casting doubt that the US is an *exceptional* country.

Edmund Burke opined in the eighteenth century that history is a pact between the dead, the living, and the unborn.[clviii] Today, America has lost its ability to harmonize its past with a hopeful future. We no longer admire great heroes from the past because they are guilty of being White and privileged. We indoctrinate the living with pseudo-intellectualism, the politics of victimology, and class envy, and we continue to pile debt onto the unborn.

We have become an ignorant and self-indulged civilization in desperate need of a wakeup call.

I began writing *An American Divorce* in 2015. At that time, my friends and family thought I was crazy to write a *revolutionary book* about America. Revolution in the United States? How could this ever happen? My friends and co-workers thought I had ventured into some faraway right-wing crazy land.

My friends and colleagues don't feel this way today.

I'm not sure how far our crystal ball will go in a world with so little predictability. This book was never meant to be a precise roadmap with exact reference points. Rather, the goal was to simply initiate a new conversation, free from the fear and judgment of the twenty-first-century thought police.

I hope it's not too late to bury the ugly monster that grew out of academia. I don't understand why "common-sense" Democrats haven't figured out they will be next in line should the traditionalist fall. Twentieth-century Republicans eventually expunged their fascist moment in the 1950s with Joseph McCarthy.

What is stopping *moderate* Democrats from doing the same today?

More importantly, why can't the Democrats and Republicans come together to defeat a common enemy that is potentially more ruthless than our worst foreign adversary?

America is an exceptional civilization because it offers hope and optimism that can be aggressively defended from tyrants. For centuries, foreign foes assumed free people would become too decadent to defend themselves. And each time, we proved them wrong.

No, we are not perfect as a country; sometimes we are the big elephant in the room that knocks everything down out of naïve intentions; sometimes we simply elect bad presidents who make terrible decisions. But even with our imperfections, the US is a great country that aspires to do good things for the world.

The intellectuals and artists have put our country into an unnecessary state of self-hatred and doubt. Maybe the hatred I witnessed at the university is rooted in arrogance. It must be difficult to be so enlightened and yet live in a country where a bricklayer with a sixth-grade education can make more money than *a tenured scholar* with a PhD in philosophy.

I *hate* what the professors have done to our great country. I am willing to risk my personal and professional reputation to defeat them. But hate is not the right path to moving away from a toxic relationship; and this reality takes us back to the first quotation in the book:

> When two people decide to get a divorce, it
> isn't that they don't understand one another, but
> a sign that they have, at last, begun to.[clix]

Hopefully, both sides can now begin to understand their marriage in a deeper context than before. Maybe this understanding will have the potential to avoid a divorce, or at the very least, make any future breakup a little less painful. America can't remain in a state of limbo as a global superpower for much longer. Our unhappy marriage is not fair to the rest of the world.

The hatred and division must end, even if the result means breaking up the United States into two separate countries.

As to potential adversaries like China and Iran: be careful what you wish for. If American patriots find a way to defeat the tyranny found in their own backyards, Chinese and Iranian patriots may follow the same revolutionary path in cities like Beijing and Tehran.

I want to close our discussion by again quoting Edmund Burke. This *man of words* famously warned of the tragic consequences when good people hide in the face of tyranny: "The only thing necessary for the triumph of evil is for good men to do nothing."[clx] We know from hindsight what followed Burke's dire warning. The eighteenth-century leftist overreach in France led to the Reign of Terror and Napoleon Bonaparte.

As Americans, we are not destined to follow the path of extremism that always seems to lead to dictators and death squads. If we can find ourselves again as a country, the *American way* will be the winner in today's global contest. Dictatorial fear and oppression will never outlast democratic hope and liberty. That is, unless the defenders of liberty stay locked in a state of guilt, apathy, and paralysis and simply choose to do nothing.

Bibliography

[i] Brooks, David. "The Morality of Selfism." *New York Times: Opinion*, January 3, 2019.

[ii] "Population estimates, quarterly." *Statistics Canada*. Last modified June 23, 2020. https://doi.org/10.25318/1710000901-eng.

[iii] "Vietnam War Casualties." *The New York Times*, January 24, 1973.

[iv] Obama, Barack. "Obama Campaign Fundraiser." Speech, San Francisco, CA, April 6, 2008.

[v] Hoffer, Eric. *The True Believer.* New York: Perennial, 2002.

[vi] Friedman, Milton. Interview by Phil Donahue. *Donahue*, Multimedia Inc., 1979.

[vii] LeTourneau, Nancy. "Hillary Clinton, Barack Obama and Saul Alinsky." *Washington Monthly*, March 15, 2016.

[viii] Alinsky, Saul. *Rules for Radicals.* Random House, 1971.

[ix] Marx, Karl and Frederich Engels. *The Communist Manifesto*. Translated by Samuel Moore. London: Workers' Educational Association, 1888.

[x] Counting Stars. "The More Than 100 Million Deaths That Communism Caused, Divided by Countries." Last Modified: December 18, 2017. https://www.outono.net/elentir/2017/12/18/the-more-than-100-million-deaths-that-communism-caused-divided-by-countries/.

[xi] Tancredo, Thomas G. *In Mortal Danger: The Battle for America's Border and Security*. Nashville: WND Books, 2006.

[xii] Tanzi, Alex and Vincent Del Giudice. "U.S. Suicide Rate Up 30% Since Start of 21st Century." *Bloomberg*, June 13, 2018. https://www.bloomberg.com/news/articles/2018-06-14/u-s-suicide-rate-up-30-since-start-of-21st-century-cdc-data.

[xiii] *A Guide to Education and No Child Left Behind*. U.S Department of Education, 2004.

[xiv] Skinner, Rebecca and Jody Feder. "Common Core State Standards: frequently asked questions." *CRS Report; R43728* (2018). Accessed: April 2020.

[xv] Patrick, John. "Democratic professors outnumber Republicans 9 to 1 at top colleges." *Washington Examiner*, January 23, 2020. https://www.washingtonexaminer.com/opinion/democratic-professors-outnumber-republicans-9-to-1-at-top-colleges.

[xvi] Brinton, Crane. *The Anatomy of Revolution.* New York: Random House, 1965.

[xvii] Chen, Grace. "Is Detroit Failing Its Students? Test Scores Say Yes" *Public School Review*, December 23, 2012

[xviii] Obama, Barack. "President Barack Obama." Interviewed by Marc Maron. WTF Podcast, June 22, 2015. Audio, 45:00. http://www.wtfpod.com/podcast/episodes/episode_613_-_president_barack_obama.

[xix] Election Results. *Charter Counter of Wayne Michigan.* Accessed July 17, 2020. https://www.waynecounty.com/elected/clerk/election-results.aspx.

[xx] Isaacson, Walter. "Benjamin Franklin Joins the Revolution." *Smithsonian Magazine*, July 31, 2003.

https://www.smithsonianmag.com/history/benjamin-franklin-joins-the-revolution-87199988/.

xxi "Census of Population: 1950 Volume II Characteristics of the Population." *United States Census Bureau*,1950 § (1953). https://www.census.gov/library/publications/1953/dec/population-vol-02.html.

xxii Mack, Julie. "Which Michigan county ranks No. 1 in births to unmarried women?" *MLive,* May 20, 2019.

xxiii Higgins, Lori. "M-STEP results for Detroit: EAA's overall proficiency less than 5%" *Detroit Free Press,* August 30, 2016.

xxiv McLanahan, Sara. "The Consequences of Single Motherhood." *The American Prospect*, December 19, 2001.

xxv Irving, Shelley K. and Tracy A. Loveless. "Dynamics of Economic Well-Being: Participation in Government Programs, 2009-2012: Who Gets Assistance?" 2015.

xxvi "Criminal Justice Fact Sheet." NAACP, Accessed: April 2020.

[xxvii] Chaudry, Ajay, Christopher Wimer, Suzanne Macartney, Lauren Frohlich, Colin Campbell, Kendall Swenson, Don Oellerich, and Susan Hauan, "Poverty in the United States: 50-Year Trends and Safety Net Impacts." 2016.

[xxviii] "2018 Crime in the United States: Expanded Homicide Data Table 6," FBI: UCR. Accessed June, 2020. Ucr.fbi.gov.

[xxix] Reynolds, David S. "Rescuing the Real Uncle Tom." *The New York Times*, June 13, 2011.

[xxx] Fitzgerald, Maggie. "Black and Hispanic unemployment is at a record low." *CNBC,* October 4, 2019.

[xxxi] Chaudry, Ajay, Christopher Wimer, Suzanne Macartney, Lauren Frohlich, Colin Campbell, Kendall Swenson, Don Oellerich, and Susan Hauan, "Poverty in the United States: 50-Year Trends and Safety Net Impacts." 2016.

[xxxii] Wolf, Zachary B. "Here's What the Green New Deal Actually Says." *CNN,* March 2, 2020.

xxxiii Holtz-Eakin, Douglas, Dan Bosch, Ben Gitis, Dan Goldbeck, and Philip Rossetti. "The Green New Deal: Scope, Scale, and Implications." *American Action Forum,* February 25, 2019.

xxxiv Fowler, Jack. "What Obama Didn't Say." *National Review*, July 22, 2013.

xxxv Ellison, Ralph and John F. Callahan. *Invisible Man.* London: Penguin Books, 2016.

xxxvi "Black Student College Graduation Rates Remain Low, But Modest Progress Begins to Show." *The Journal of Blacks in Higher Education*, June 23, 2020. Jbhe.com.

xxxvii King, Martin Luther Jr. "I Have a Dream." Speech, Washington, DC, August 28, 1963.

xxxviii "U.S. Census Bureau QuickFacts: United States." *Census Bureau QuickFacts*, Accessed: April, 2020.

xxxix "Howard Hughes Dies at 70 On Flight to Texas Hospital." *The New York Times*, April 6, 1976.

[xl] "U.S. Census Bureau QuickFacts: United States." *Census Bureau QuickFacts*. Accessed April, 2020.

[xli] Statista, Presidential Election Exit Polls: Share of votes by ethnicity U.S. 2020, November 9, 2020.

[xlii] Leila, Fidel, "Majority of Muslims Voted for Biden, but Trump Got more, Not Less." Kuow Puget Sound Public Radio, December 4, 2020

[xliii] "U.S. Census Bureau QuickFacts: United States." Census Bureau QuickFacts. Accessed April, 2020.

[xliv] "Most Dangerous Countries in the World 2020." World Population Review. Accessed July 17, 2020. https://worldpopulationreview.com/country-rankings/most-dangerous-countries

[xlv] Reilly, Katie. "Here Are All the Times Donald Trump Insulted Mexico." *Time*, August 31, 2016.

[xlvi] Reilly, Katie. "Here Are All the Times Donald Trump Insulted Mexico." *Time*, August 31, 2016.

xlvii Gonzalez-Barrera, Ana and Jens Manuel Krogstad. "What We Know about Illegal Immigration from Mexico." *Pew Research Center,* June 28, 2019.

xlviii Lipka, Michael. "Muslims and Islam: Key Findings in the U.S. and around the World." *Pew Research Center,* August 9, 2017.

xlix "The World's Muslims: Religion, Politics and Society." *Pew Research Center*, April 30, 2013. Pewforum.org.

l Abulafia, Anna Sapir. "The Abrahamic Religions." *The British Library,* December 7, 2018.

li "Sunnis and Shia: Islam's Ancient Schism." *BBC News,* January 4, 2016.

lii "Muhammad: Legacy of a Prophet. Life of Muhammad." *PBS.* 2002.

liii The Qur'an. [Sahih International, 2:275-279].

liv The Qur'an. [Sahih International, 9:29].

lv The Editorial Board. "Visas for Hong Kong." *The Wall Street Journal*, May 30, 2020. Wsj.com.

[lvi] The Editorial Board. "Visas for Hong Kong." *The Wall Street Journal*, May 30, 2020. Wsj.com.

[lvii] Sales, Ben. "America's 7.5 million Jews are older, whiter and more liberal than the country as a whole." *Jewish Telegraphic Agency,* October 7, 2019.

[lviii] "An examination of the 2016 electorate, based on validated voters." *Pew Research Center,* August 9, 2018.

[lix] Wang, Wendy. "The Link Between a College Education and a Lasting Marriage." *Pew Research Center,* December 2, 2015.

[lx] Reilly, Katie. "Read Hillary Clinton's 'Basket of Deplorables' Remarks About Donald Trump Supporters." *Time,* September 10, 2016.

[lxi] Associated Press. "Bush offers up 'ownership society.'" *NBC News*, February 2, 2002. http://www.nbcnews.com/id/6902224/ns/politics-state_of_the_union/t/bush-offers-ownership-society/#.XwS23ShKiBs.

[lxii] Zarroli, Jim. "The U.S. Was Already Deep in Debt. This Year's Deficit Will Be 'Mind Boggling'." *NPR*, March 30, 2020.

[lxiii] Chappel, Bill. "Supreme Court Declares Same-Sex Marriage Legal in All 50 States." *NPR,* June 26, 2015.

[lxiv] "Gender Nation Glossary." *Refinery29*, June 1, 2018. https://www.refinery29.com/en-us/lgbtq-definitions-gender-sexuality-terms.

[lxv] Baculinao, Eric. "Why Is China Raising the Prospect of Same-Sex Marriage?" *NBC News,* January 7, 2020.

[lxvi] Lewis, Sophie. "Putin Wants to Ban Gay Marriage in a Revised Version of the Russian Constitution." *CBS News,* March 3, 2020.

[lxvii] *Obergefell v. Hodges*, 576 U.S. 644 (2015).

[lxviii] *Obergefell v. Hodges*, 576 U.S. 644 (2015).

[lxix] Rudgard, Olivia. "Only Two Thirds of Generation Z Identify as 'Exclusively Heterosexual'." *The Telegraph,* July 4, 2018.

[lxx] Wilhelm, Amara Das. "A Timeline of Gay World History." *GALVA-108,* April 14, 2020.

lxxi "The truth about sexuality in ancient Greece and Rome." *Gay Star News*, October 1, 2016. https://www.gaystarnews.com/article/truth-about-sexuality-ancient-greece-and-rome261012/.

lxxii Strachan, Maxwell. "The Behind-The-Scenes Story of 'Brokeback Mountain,' 10 Years Later." *HuffPost*, December 11, 2015.

lxxiii Elnaiem, Mohammed. "In the McCarthy Era, to Be Black Was to Be Red." *JSTOR Daily*, November 13, 2019. https://daily.jstor.org/in-the-mccarthy-era-to-be-black-was-to-be-red/.

lxxiv Lim, Kay M. and Julie Kracov. "The Lavender Scare: How the Federal Government Purged Gay Employees." *CBS News*, June 9, 2019.

lxxv Anderson, Hans Christian. *The Emperor's New Clothes*. C.A. Reitzel, 1837.

lxxvi Harvey, Matt. "Sen. Joe McCarthy's Startling Morphine Source." *The Fix*, May 13, 2013.

lxxvii Harvey, Matt. "Sen. Joe McCarthy's Startling Morphine Source." *The Fix*, May 13, 2013.

lxxviii Schlesinger, Arthur Meier. *The Coming of the New Deal, 1933-1935.* Boston: Houghton Mifflin, 2003.

lxxix Schlesinger, Arthur Meier. *The Coming of the New Deal, 1933-1935.* Boston: Houghton Mifflin, 2003.

lxxx Davis, Alyssa and Lawrence Mishel. "CEO Pay Continues to Rise as Typical Workers Are Paid Less." *Economic Policy Institute,* June 12, 2014.

lxxxi Davis, Alyssa and Lawrence Mishel. "CEO Pay Continues to Rise as Typical Workers Are Paid Less." *Economic Policy Institute,* June 12, 2014.

lxxxii Elliot, Larry. "World's 26 Richest People Own as Much as Poorest 50%, Says Oxfam." *The Guardian,* January 21, 2019.

lxxxiii Elkins, Kathleen. "Here's How Much Americans Have Saved for Retirement at Different Ages." *CNBC,* January 23, 2020.

lxxxiv Snider, Susannah. "Tax-Filing in 2020: What is My Tax Bracket?" *U.S. News & World Report,* November 8, 2019.

lxxxv "Topic No. 409 Capital Gains and Losses." *Internal Revenue Service,* February 11, 2020.

lxxxvi Fletcher, Christine. "Eight Things You Need to Know About The Death Tax Before You Die." *Forbes Magazine,* May 20, 2019.

lxxxvii "SEC Adopts Rule for Pay Ratio Disclosure." *U.S. Securities and Exchange Commission*, August 5, 2015. https://www.sec.gov/news/pressrelease/2015-160.html.

lxxxviii "Remarks by the President at a Campaign Event in Roanoke, Virginia." *National Archives and Records Administration*, July 13, 2012.

lxxxix Harris, Ainsley. "Jeff Bezos Made 1.2 Million Times the Median Amazon Employee in 2017." *Fast Company,* April 19, 2018.

xc Rogers, Taylor Nicole. "Wealth Tax Explainer: Why Bernie Sanders, Elizabeth Warren and Billionaires like George Soros Alike Are Calling for a Specialized Tax on the Ultra-Wealthy." *Business Insider,* September 24, 2019.

xci Rogers, Taylor Nicole. "Wealth Tax Explainer: Why Bernie Sanders, Elizabeth Warren and Billionaires like George Soros Alike Are Calling for a Specialized Tax on the Ultra-Wealthy." *Business Insider,* September 24, 2019.

[xcii] Rogers, Taylor Nicole. "Wealth Tax Explainer: Why Bernie Sanders, Elizabeth Warren and Billionaires like George Soros Alike Are Calling for a Specialized Tax on the Ultra-Wealthy." *Business Insider,* September 24, 2019.

[xciii] Byrnes, Hristina. "U.S. Leads Among Countries That Spend the Most on Public Health Care." *USA Today*, April 11, 2019.

[xciv] Coppess, Jonathan. "1930s Dust Bowl: Government Policy Climate Farming Methods." *AgFax,* October 25, 2019.

[xcv] French, Sally. "The Huge Floating Island of Trash in the Pacific Ocean Is Now Twice the Size of Texas." *MarketWatch,* March 23, 2018.

[xcvi] Newport, Frank. "Americans Greatly Overestimate Percent Gay, Lesbian in U.S." *Gallup,* May 21, 2015.

[xcvii] "Red" states are defined as U.S. states who voted for Donald Trump in 2016. "Blue" states are defined as U.S. states who voted for Hillary Clinton in 2016.

[xcviii] Muro, Mark and Jacob Whiton. "America Has Two Economies—and They're Diverging Fast." *Brookings,* September 19, 2019.

[xcix] Cummings, Michelle. "Who Are the Givers? The Northeast Subsidizes Federal Spending." *Rockefeller Institute of Government*, January 25, 2019.

[c] Cummings, Michelle. "Who Are the Givers? The Northeast Subsidizes Federal Spending." *Rockefeller Institute of Government*, January 25, 2019.

[ci] Schultz, Laura. "Who Are the Getters? The Federal Workforce and Low-Income States Get the Most." *Rockefeller Institute of Government*, February 1, 2019.

[cii] Schultz, Laura. "Who Are the Getters? The Federal Workforce and Low-Income States Get the Most." *Rockefeller Institute of Government*, February 1, 2019.

[ciii] Schultz, Laura. "Who Are the Getters? The Federal Workforce and Low-Income States Get the Most." *Rockefeller Institute of Government*, February 1, 2019.

[civ] Schultz, Laura. "Who Are the Getters? The Federal Workforce and Low-Income States Get the Most." *Rockefeller Institute of Government*, February 1, 2019.

[cv] Kilgore, Ed. "Trump Tax Bill Hammers New York and California." *Intelligencer, New York Magazine*, November 2, 2017.

[cvi] "U.S. Census Bureau QuickFacts: Arkansas; Louisiana; Mississippi; United States." *Census Bureau QuickFacts*. Accessed April 2020.

[cvii] "U.S. Census Bureau QuickFacts: Connecticut; Vermont; Massachusetts; United States." *Census Bureau QuickFacts*. Accessed April, 2020.

[cviii] Harrington, John. "There Are 18.2 Million Veterans in the US. Which State Is Home to the Most of Them?" *USA Today,* July 4, 2019.

[cix] Reilly, Katie. "Read Hillary Clinton's 'Basket of Deplorables' Remarks About Donald Trump Supporters." *Time,* September 10, 2016.

[cx] Kelly, Martin. "Which State Seceded First During the American Civil War?" *ThoughtCo.,* February 11, 2019. https://www.thoughtco.com/order-of-secession-during-civil-war-104535.

[cxi] Kelly, Martin. "Which State Seceded First During the American Civil War?" *ThoughtCo.,* February 11, 2019. https://www.thoughtco.com/order-of-secession-during-civil-war-104535.

[cxii] Beckert, Sven. "Empire of Cotton." *The Atlantic,* December 12, 2014.

[cxiii] Hawes, Robert F. *One Nation, Indivisible?: A Study of Secession and the Constitution.* Palo Alto: Fultus Corporation, 2006.

[cxiv] Hawes, Robert F. *One Nation, Indivisible?: A Study of Secession and the Constitution.* Palo Alto: Fultus Corporation, 2006.

[cxv] U.S. Constitution. Article IV. Sec. 3. Cl. 1. https://www.senate.gov/civics/constitution_item/constitution.htm#a4.

[cxvi] Texas v. White, 74 US 700. Supreme Court, 1869.

[cxvii] Rogers, Abby. "Sorry Secessionists, Justice Scalia Won't Help You Out." *Business Insider,* November 15, 2012.

[cxviii] "Article V, U.S. Constitution." *National Archives and Records Administration.* Accessed: May, 2020.

[cxix] U.S. Constitution, Article V. *National Archives.*

[cxx] Coyle, Marcia. "Scalia, Ginsburg Offer Amendments to the Constitution." *National Law Journal,* April 17, 2014.

cxxi America's Founding Documents: The Constitution. National Archives, Washington DC. https://www.archives.gov/founding-docs

cxxii Moran, Chris. "The Curious Story of the Confederate 'Greyback'." *Greenwich Sentinel*, February 12, 2016.

cxxiii Wolf, Stephen. "Daily Kos Election Presents the 2016 Presidential Election Results by Congressional District." *Daily Kos*, January 30, 2017.

cxxiv Brinton, Crane. *The Anatomy of Revolution.* New York: Random House, 1965.

cxxv Brinton, Crane. *The Anatomy of Revolution.* New York: Random House, 1965.

cxxvi Brinton, Crane. *The Anatomy of Revolution.* New York: Random House, 1965.

cxxvii Hoffer, Eric. *The True Believer.* New York: Perennial, 2002.

cxxviii Hoffer, Eric. *The True Believer.* New York: Perennial, 2002.

cxxix Hoffer, Eric. *The True Believer.* New York: Perennial, 2002.

cxxx Hoffer, Eric. *The True Believer.* New York: Perennial, 2002.

[cxxxi] Hoffer, Eric. *The True Believer.* New York: Perennial, 2002.

[cxxxii] Brinton, Crane. *The Anatomy of Revolution.* New York: Random House, 1965.

[cxxxiii] Brinton, Crane. *The Anatomy of Revolution.* New York: Random House, 1965.

[cxxxiv] Hoff, Madison, "Many of the Founding Fathers were incredibly wealthy. Here's a look at some of their fortunes." Business Insider, July 4, 2020.

[cxxxv] Alinsky, Saul. *Rules for Radicals.* Random House, 1971.

[cxxxvi] Frank, Robert. "Hillary is the favorite among millionaire voters: Survey." *CNBC,* May 6, 2015.

[cxxxvii] Dalton, Sam. "Chelsea Clinton's millions and the American aristocracy." *World Socialist Web Site,* January 10, 2020.

[cxxxviii] Fisher, Anthony L. "Elizabeth Warren's advice to parents of kids in struggling public schools reeks of privilege." *Business Insider,* December 19, 2019.

cxxxix Ivanova, Polina, Maria Tsvetkova, Ilya Zhegulev and Luke Baker. "What Hunter Biden did on the board of Ukrainian energy company Burisma." *Reuters*, October 18, 2019.

cxl Parker, Maggie. "The 12 Most Unique College Courses Offered Around the U.S." *Bestlife,* July, 2018.

cxli Brinton, Crane. *The Anatomy of Revolution.* New York: Random House, 1965.

cxlii Alinsky, Saul. *Rules for Radicals.* Random House, 1971.

cxliii Jurecic, Quinta. "Why the Kavanaugh Confirmation Still Haunts Us." *The Atlantic,* September 18, 2019.

cxliv Matousek, Mark. "Elon Musk says you still don't need a college degree to work at Tesla. Here's what he looks for in job applicants instead." *Business Insider*, January 8, 2020.

cxlv Brinton, Crane. *The Anatomy of Revolution.* New York: Random House, 1965.

cxlvi Hoffer, Eric. *The True Believer.* New York: Perennial, 2002.

cxlix Rushe, Dominic. "Detroit becomes largest US city to file for bankruptcy in historic 'low point.'" *The Guardian,* July 18, 2013.

cl Klinefelter, Quinn. "Detroit's Big Comeback: Out of Bankruptcy, A Rebirth." *NPR Morning Edition,* December 18, 2018.

cli Brinton, Crane. *The Anatomy of Revolution.* New York: Random House, 1965.

clii Hoffer, Eric. *The True Believer.* New York: Perennial, 2002.

cliii Hoffer, Eric. *The True Believer.* New York: Perennial, 2002.

cliv Hoffer, Eric. *The True Believer.* New York: Perennial, 2002.

clv Hoffer, Eric. *The True Believer.* New York: Perennial, 2002.

clvi Devlin, Kat, Laura Silver, and Christine Huang. "U.S. Views of China Increasingly Negative Amid Coronavirus Outbreak." *Pew Research Center,* April 21, 2020.

clvii Dilanian, Ken. "American universities are a soft target for China's spies, say U.S. intelligence officials." *NBC News,* February 2, 2020.

[clviii] Burke, Edmund. "Reflections on the Revolution in France," 1790. *The Works of the Right Honorable Edmund Burke,* vol. 3, p. 359 (1899).

[clix] Rowland, Helen. *Reflections of a Bachelor Girl.* New York: Dodge Publishing Company, 1909.

[clx] Attributed to Edmund Burke. "Thoughts on the Cause of the Present Discontents," 82-83 (1770) in: *Select Works of Edmund Burke, vol. 1, p. 146. Liberty Fund edition, 1999.*